# Hopi KACHINA Spirit of Life

Edited by Dorothy K. Washburn

*Dedicated to the Hopi Tricentennial, 1680-1980*

PUBLISHED BY
THE CALIFORNIA ACADEMY OF SCIENCES,
IN CONJUNCTION WITH
THE EXHIBITION
"HOPI KACHINA: SPIRIT OF LIFE"

DISTRIBUTED BY
THE UNIVERSITY OF WASHINGTON PRESS,
SEATTLE AND LONDON.

Library of Congress Catalog Card Number
79-54647
ISBN 0-295-95751-4

Cover: Kwa (Eagle Kachina) No. 138

All photography by Susan Middleton
except as follows:

Color Plate 8 and No. 10:
Peabody Museum, Harvard University
Photographs by Hillel Burger

Color Plate 16:
The Gallery Wall

No. 11:
Museum of Northern Arizona
Photograph by Mark Middleton

Fig. 66:
California Academy of Sciences
Photograph by Lloyd Ullberg

Printed in the United States of America by
Phelps/Schaefer Litho-Graphics Co., San Francisco.
Typeset by Terry Robinson & Co., San Francisco.
Catalogue design by Gordon Chun.
Logotype by Kevin O'Farrell.
Distributed by the University of Washington Press,
Seattle and London.

# Contents

# Foreword

The high desert of northern Arizona which spreads east of the San Francisco Mountains and the Grand Canyon and south of Monument Valley is a place of vast vistas and immense sky. Little rain falls there and the wind is often strong. It is not an easy place; yet within it, on and around three fingerlike mesas, the Native Americans we call the Hopi live and have lived for many centuries. One of their settlements is said to have been inhabited without interruption for nearly nine hundred years, longer than any other place in the United States.

The people called the Hopi have adapted to their stern environment, maintaining an intimate relationship with the elements of their natural world which enables them to survive. They are effective farmers where agriculture would seem to be impossible, carefully husbanding limited resources of water and tillable soil, raising the beans, corn and squash of their ancestors and the peaches and melons they obtained from the Spaniards. The Hopi are talented craftsmen and by nature they are generous and sharing, industrious and conservative.

The Hopi people are humble and respectful of their world and of the spirits which control the elements which make it habitable. Those spirits, the kachinas, are with them intimately through half of the year, in sacred places called kivas where there is fasting and singing and praying, and outside in plazas with ceremonial dances and celebration. This exhibition is about the Hopi and the kachinas.

We are indebted to many who made "Hopi Kachina: Spirit of Life" possible. Nathaniel Owings has been intensely interested in the Hopi and Native American Puebloans of the Rio Grande valley for many years, and recently gave his substantial collection of kachina dolls to the California Academy of Sciences. Mr. Owings first proposed this exhibition and his unbridled enthusiasm has been an important factor in its creation. The National Endowment for the Humanities provided matching grants for planning and implementation of the exhibition.

A number of distinguished Hopi leaders and scholars participated in a planning conference in San Francisco and have since continued their active assistance and support as consultants and contributors to this catalogue and other exhibition-related publications. The cooperation of the many institutions and individuals who loaned kachinas and other artifacts is deeply appreciated, as is the contribution of all those who produced the exhibition. The following list is not complete, nor is it adequate, but to all who made "Hopi Kachina: Spirit of Life" possible, we are grateful.

George Lindsay
Director
California Academy of Sciences

LENDERS TO THE EXHIBITION:

American Museum of Natural History
Arizona State Museum
Carnegie Museum of Natural History
Denver Museum of Natural History
Field Museum of Natural History
The Gallery Wall
Heard Museum
Maxwell Museum of Anthropology
Museum of the American Indian, Heye Foundation
Museum of New Mexico
Museum of Northern Arizona
National Museum of Natural History, Smithsonian Institution
Peabody Museum of Archaeology and Ethnology
School of American Research
Southwest Museum, Los Angeles
University Museum, University of Pennsylvania
Mr. and Mrs. John Connelly
Mr. and Mrs. Grant Winther

SPONSORS OF THE EXHIBITION:

California Academy of Sciences
National Endowment for the Humanities
Mr. and Mrs. Thomas Tilton
Santa Fe Railway Company
Fireman's Fund Insurance Company Foundation
Pinewood Foundation
The Hearst Foundation
Transamerica Corporation
Mr. and Mrs. Nathaniel Owings

CONSULTANTS:

Mr. Robert Ames
Mr. Bob Black
Mr. Moris Burge
Mrs. Carlotta Connelly
Mr. John Connelly
Dr. Bertha Dutton
Mr. Fred Kabotie
Mr. Michael Kabotie
Mr. Hartman Lomawaima
Mr. Nathaniel Owings
Mr. Emory Sekaquaptewa
Mr. Ben Setima
Mr. Watson Smith
Mr. Terrance Talaswaima
Mrs. Barbara Winther
Mr. Barton Wright
Mr. Ben Elkus
Mr. Robert Elkus
Museum Board of the Hopi Cultural Center Museum

PRODUCTION STAFF:

Dr. Dorothy K. Washburn, Project Director
Ms. Patricia M. Burke, Project Coordinator
Mr. Kevin O'Farrell, Project Designer
Ms. Leslie Flint, Catalog Production
Mr. Gordon Chun, Catalog Designer
Ms. Susan Middleton, Catalog Photographer
Mr. Robert Bjorkland, Chairman, Exhibits Department
Staff: Exhibits Department, Wood Shop, Instrument Shop
Dr. David Parker, Audio-visual Production
Mr. Hans Halberstadt, Audio-visual Photography

# Prologue

In our youth, old men of the day reiterated the teaching of prophecy that a day will come to pass when new generations of Hopi will become as the ears and tongues for the old. We understood this to mean education in the ways of the white man in his schools so that we may help our people find a smoother path in the world dominated by the white man. In a society bound by oral tradition, such as Hopi, where the semblance of the past, present and the future hangs on the spoken word, the ability to listen and to speak takes on special qualities. Ritual symbolism and the effects of special times and places for the exchange of ideas by oral means were important elements to speaking and listening. Little did we realize then that this moral duty imposed by the prophecy would transcend these ordinary modes for the exchange of ideas, and would, indeed, lead us to such complex processes as the visual subtleties of form, color and material.

It is both a pleasure and a privilege to collaborate with the Science Museum of the California Academy of Sciences in the production of an exhibit that hopes to bring the Hopi world to the outside onlooker. If seeing is believing, then it might be suggested as a corollary that listening with the heart and mind to what is behind the things of Hopi is understanding. In this modern day the Hopi people find it appropriate to commemorate certain events in their past by designating 1980 as the year of celebration. While this celebration is to renew the spirit of Hopiism for the Hopi people, it is our hope that this exhibit will help carry this spirit to the rest of the world.

Emory Sekaquaptewa
Department of Anthropology
University of Arizona

# Introduction

Ever since the idea for an exhibit about the Hopi was born several years ago, our Hopi friends have generously been giving of themselves and their culture. It is now our turn to open to you a window on their world.

As in any culture, there are certain things, such as very sacred ideas and paraphernalia, that belong to the Hopi themselves. Nevertheless, there are many public aspects of a culture which carry the essence of that culture, and thus serve to render each group unique and identifiable as a separate cultural entity. Our Hopi consultants have suggested that we focus upon the kachinas (*katsinam*) and their role in transmitting the prayers and hopes for continued prosperity to the deities above. Thus, we are presenting but a fraction of the whole of Hopi thought and material assemblage, but it is one that will help you to understand better how the Hopi relate to their environment and to each other.

In a museum exhibit it is very difficult to describe the essence and spirit of one culture to a person from another culture. Even with modern technological apparatus for recreating sound, smell and atmosphere, nothing can substitute for actual presence. Nevertheless, in this exhibit we have attempted to capture some of the special senses one feels upon entering another cultural world.

The exhibit begins with an audio-visual introduction to the windswept, arid mesas and farmfields of the Hopi Indians in northeastern Arizona and introduces the kachinas, supernatural messengers who mediate between the harsh realities of Arizona's environmental limitations and the daily needs of the Hopi people.

Kachinas begin their work of prayers and good thoughts in kivas. We take you past the hatchway of one of these underground ceremonial chambers so you may listen to the sounds of kachinas practicing songs they will sing at the public dances. All of Hopi life is a complex orchestration of the spiritual with the secular, and even daily tasks, such as farming or marriage, are overlaid with symbolic enrichment that gives them a sacred aura. The days of preparation for these public displays of prayers sung and offerings shared are among the most important for they move Hopi hearts from mundane worries toward a collective uplift of the spirit of the whole Hopi community.

The kachinas, whose prayers are concerned with fertility and growth, appear in February at Powamu (*Powamuya*) to open the growing season and leave in July at Niman (*Niman*) just prior to the harvest.In the exhibit two models scaled to the size of kachina dolls portray the kachinas as they appear at Powamu and Niman. Between these two events, many dances, clowns, weddings and long days in the fields are explained through photographs and artifacts.

To close the exhibit we have invited the Hopi themselves to talk with you about their present life and future hopes. We hope that this exhibit will not only bring you closer to the spirit of the Hopi people but also be a fitting contribution to their celebration of the Pueblo Tricentennial—300 years of freedom from Spanish rule.

The catalogue is designed to provide supplementary information about aspects of artifacts or ideas in the exhibit. Each of the articles represents the author's own research conclusions or impressions from his or her personal knowledge of the Hopi.

Of paramount importance was the close cooperation we received from the Hopi people during the development of the exhibit. With their help in procuring permission for photography, in borrowing artifacts and in counseling how best to explain ideas and items, we have endeavored to produce an exhibit that will be as comfortable for the Hopi as it is interesting and informative for the American public.

Hopi was an unwritten language when the first ethnologists began recording Hopi activities. In the absence of dictionaries, these investigators simply wrote down what they heard. Naturally each word list varied and this has resulted in a myriad of different spellings for kachinas, villages and other items of material culture. We have attempted to rectify this situation by having Emory Sekaquaptewa, a native Hopi speaker from the University of Arizona, compile a word list of all Hopi words used in the exhibit and catalogue. After the first use of a Hopi word in the text, it is spelled as correctly pronounced by Third Mesa Hopi in parentheses after the common Anglo spelling. For consistency in the Anglo spelling we have followed Harold Colton's spelling of kachinas (1959). In many cases it may seem that the Hopi word bears little resemblance to its Anglo rendering, but remember that this is a consequence of years of misspelling and mispronunciation which became a habit and thus in our minds "correct."

It is difficult as a *bahana (pahaana)* (the Hopi word for white persons) to reset our thinking about another culture. Old habits and values die slowly. But if we listen with our hearts and minds to the Hopi as they tell us about their life through the visuals and artifacts in our exhibit, we can expand our appreciation of the uniqueness of another culture. Perhaps a key to understanding the Hopi lies in a comment by one of our Hopi friends: "Hopis have always been very good at preserving ideas, but very poor at at preserving things." The form, color and material of the artifacts are all visual representations of concepts basic to Hopi life. The Hopi people have preserved these lifeways and values despite centuries of exposure to the pressures of the dominant Spanish and American cultures. Indeed, the Hopi are America's oldest continuously surviving culture. In this period of change and exhaustion of our national spirit and resources, a culture which has persevered certainly deserves our considered attention.

Dorothy K. Washburn
Chairman, Department of Anthropology
California Academy of Sciences

# THE PREHISTORIC AND HISTORIC
# OCCUPATION OF THE
# HOPI MESAS

# by E. Charles Adams and Deborah Hull

The history of the area we know today as the Hopi mesas is as yet incompletely understood. The Hopi mesas area has been used by man for at least 5000 and perhaps for 10,000 or more years (Gumerman 1965:79-80; 1969-313-317). But our direct knowledge of the area prior to A.D. 700 is derived only from sparse surface remains of past cultures, and must be largely extrapolated from archaeological work done nearby (Gumerman 1968, 1969; Gumerman, Westfall and Weed 1972). Our knowledge of the period A.D. 700 to 1700 stems primarily from work done in the eastern part of the Hopi mesas by the Peabody Museum's Awatovi Expeditions. The historic period from 1540 to 1700 is known from the archaeological investigation of the village of Awatovi, supplemented by a few written documents. The period 1700 to 1875 is known a little better through Spanish, Mexican and early Anglo chronicles and recent excavations at the village of Walpi (*Walpi*), founded in 1690 and still occupied. Only the last century is well documented, and much of this period prior to 1930 is known due to the efforts of a few hardy ethnographers and avid photographers.

Evidence for the first 8000 years is meager, reflecting the nature of the subsistence of the people, which consisted of gathering locally available wild plants and hunting animals as they were encountered. In the latter stages of this time period, known as the Archaic, domesticated maize, or corn, was introduced from Mexico. This introduction eventually led to profound changes in the lifeway of the hunters and gatherers of the area.

In 1927 Southwestern archaeologists gathered at Pecos Pueblo near Santa Fe and established a chronology for prehistoric events extending through a series of periods. These periods were named Basketmaker and Pueblo and numbered sequentially. This chronology begins ca. A.D. 1 and extends to the present. The earliest people in this chronological sequence in the vicinity of the Hopi mesas are the Basketmaker people, named from the beautiful baskets they made. The reason their remains are relatively abundant is that they often built their houses in dry caves, or rock-shelters, which preserved their material remains. These people inhabited the four corners region of the Southwest, where the states of Utah, Colorado, New Mexico and Arizona touch corners, from the first century A.D. to A.D. 700. Remains of maize and squash testify to their increasing reliance on domesticated

# Prehistoric Period

Fig. 1. A view of Walpi, First Mesa, from the northeast photographed by A. C. Vroman in 1897. The absence of electricity and plumbing continues to this day. Courtesy of the Los Angeles County Museum of Natural History V-510.

foodstuffs, though they still depended primarily on hunted and gathered food.

These people lived in shallow pit houses, or houses built in pits dug to a depth of one to two feet. The superstructure of these houses was constructed of jacal, from the Mexican Nahuatl word referring to pole walls chinked with mud. Food was stored in pits excavated into the dirt floors and walls of the houses, or in separate cists, which are storage pits with their own jacal superstructure. Village size was typically two to five pit houses.

Around A.D. 500, the people acquired the knowledge of how to bake clay into pottery. These pottery vessels were more efficient for cooking and storing. People began constructing more elaborate pit houses averaging three feet in depth, with benches and formal entryways. Villages became larger. By A.D. 700 beans were added to the diet of the people; cotton and turkeys were introduced.

This period is the first to leave substantial evidence in the Hopi mesas area and is represented by the village Jeddito 264, which was excavated in the 1930s by the Peabody Museum's Awatovi Expedition. Jeddito 264 lies on a spur of rock extending from the east edge of Antelope Mesa. This village was first inhabited about A.D. 700 at a time when the population in and around the Hopi mesas was rapidly expanding. The people of Jeddito 264 must have farmed the valley below and depended on nearby springs for their water supply. The people lived in pit houses which had features borrowed from their neighbors to the north and to the south. This mixture or melting pot of ideas and people has continued to characterize the Hopi mesas area throughout its history.

During the early stages of the following Pueblo I period, pit houses continued to be used, ranging up to eight feet deep. At this same time aboveground rooms, constructed first of jacal and then of masonry, first appeared. Initially, these rooms were used only for storage; then they were used for summer habitation. People eventually left their pit houses altogether in favor of the aboveground rooms. These rooms were joined and they formed room blocks, thus giving rise to the Spanish term "pueblo" for this and subsequent periods. Pit houses, however, were not completely abandoned, but served as ceremonial chambers, not too dissimilar to the kivas employed by the Hopi of today.

This characterization of the early Pueblo period applies to the Hopi mesas area. Village size increased little from the Basketmaker Period. Agricultural dependence continued to increase, comprising 50 percent or more of the diet. This accounts for the stability of the population and the more lengthy occupation of the villages.

During the next period, Pueblo II, which dates from about A.D. 900 to 1100, the masonry villages increased in number but decreased in size. These pueblos usually surrounded a plaza area in which the kivas were built. Except for the age and technological level of these villages, their appearance is remarkably similar to that of the modern Hopi village. In the Hopi mesas area the

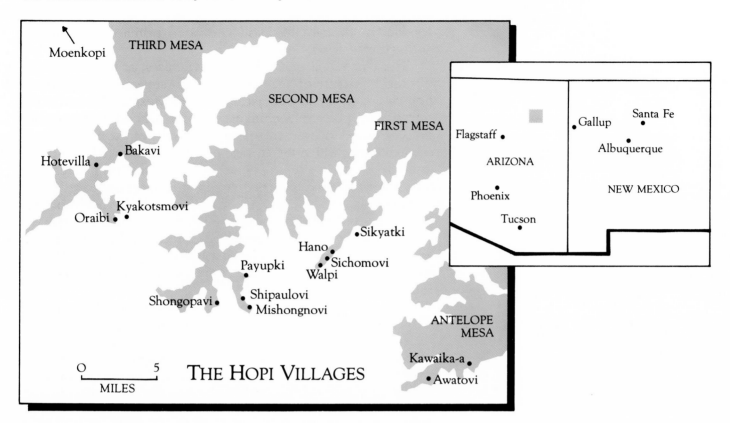

THE HOPI VILLAGES

Fig. 2. Northeastern Arizona.

valley locations were abandoned in favor of the mesa tops. With this movement away from the farming area, the need arose for houses near the fields which were used only during the summer and fall months. The changing pattern in settlement may reflect an adaptation to the protracted period of drier weather or just a change in the season when the moisture falls.

The following Pueblo III period, A.D. 1100-1300, witnessed substantial changes in population on the Colorado Plateau. These changes were probably caused by a climate which continued to deteriorate in terms of its reliability for agriculture. Throughout this period people clustered into fewer but larger villages, many of which developed on the Hopi mesas and surrounding area. Strong attractions to this area must have been the dependable springs and the relatively large tracts of farmable land. As the thirteenth century drew to a close, most of the Colorado Plateau was abandoned, with the people withdrawing to the well-watered regions, such as the Rio Grande River and the Hopi mesas. The villages occupied during this period and the later centuries in the vicinity of the Hopi mesas show remarkable increases in population—some reaching from several hundred to over a thousand rooms in size.

These fourteenth century sites are almost identical in size and features to the modern Hopi villages. Indeed, the village of Oraibi (*Orayvi*) and the historic village of Awatovi were both founded prior to 1300.

The above outline reveals a continuity in culture over a millenium. The ability to survive in the sometimes harsh, arid land of the Colorado Plateau is no doubt due in large part to the closeness with which the people lived with their environment and their ability to adjust to its long-term changes, as well as its short-term fluctuations.

# The Ancestral Hopi Period: 1350-1540

During Pueblo III in the Hopi mesas area there were forty-seven pueblos inhabited. Thirty-six of these were abandoned between 1275 and 1300. The eleven remaining plus the three villages founded after 1300 represent human occupation of this area during the Pueblo IV period. Although there were fewer villages, they were much larger than in the previous period. Thus in the period corresponding to the "Great Drought" (1276-1299), in which population declined and abandonment of large areas occurred over much of the Southwest, there was an increase in population in the Hopi area.

Why did people remain in or move to the Hopi area in a time of extreme environmental stress? It was due primarily to the permanent and abundant water supply in the area in combination with the arrival of the kachina (katsina) cult, facilitating development of larger, more complex villages capable of self-support through more efficient exploitation of the local resources. Hack (1942) provides details as to why there is such an abundant supply of water in a seemingly arid environment. During times of drought, the abundance of moisture in the sand dunes has made them an attractive and feasible dry-farming supplement to the flood-water farming which characterizes the area. Also, when drainages become entrenched, dry-land farming may become the only alternative for growing adequate crops.

The Pueblo IV sites, because of their spectacular size and their place in the lore of the local inhabitants, have been the focus of archaeological work in the Hopi area. In 1895 Fewkes (1898) excavated in Sikyatki and tested Awatovi and Homolovi. Hough (1903, 1918) excavated in Pink Arrow, Nesuftanga and Chakpahu on Antelope Mesa in 1901. In 1929 Hargrave (1931a) tested Kokopnyama on Antelope Mesa. The Peabody Museum's Awatovi Expedition from 1935 to 1939 excavated in Awatovi and Kawaika-a, both also on Antelope Mesa (Brew 1941). Unfortunately, most of this work has not been published.

The Pueblo IV sites range from about fifty rooms to over a thousand rooms. Villages of this size require a more complex social organization and probably reflect incipient chiefdoms (Sahlins 1962:170-177). This can be inferred by the presence of water-control systems which require more group activity and supervision. The latter would indicate a need for a more centralized authority. In times of stress, as this might have been, the kivas may have functioned as redistribution centers for food. The centralized authority, incipient stratification of society and the redistributive function of the kiva are present in modern Hopi villages and evidently appear in association with the kachina cult in the fourteenth century.

The architecture of these Pueblo IV villages is quite similar to that of the modern villages. They all have central plazas surrounded on all sides by rooms or walls. The room blocks are composed of stone walls cemented with adobe and usually plastered. They are usually multiple stories and contain both habitation and storage rooms. For each habitation room there are two or more storage rooms and an outside work area. There are also specific rooms called mealing rooms for the communal grinding of maize. The kivas are placed in the central plaza, usually oriented to the northwest. These kivas are rectangular, give the appearance of being subterranean, often occur in groups of two or three and are virtually indistinguishable from modern Hopi kivas (Smith 1972:123-125). On Antelope Mesa and Second Mesa there are outcrops of subbituminous coal in the Toreva Formation which were mined during Pueblo IV and used for heating houses and firing pottery (Hack 1942a:7).

The link between these Pueblo IV villages and the modern Hopi can be traced through the legends from the oral tradition of the Hopi and the unique kiva murals uncovered at Awatovi and Kawaika-a.

Decorative painting of rooms and kivas first appeared in late Pueblo II in the Ackmen-Lowry area in southwestern Colorado and the Chaco area in northwestern New Mexico, becoming somewhat more diversified in Pueblo III. These murals occurred mostly in kivas, were bichrome (either black designs on a white background or white designs on a red background) and had geometric motifs (Smith 1952:53-68). During Pueblo IV a sudden change in murals occurred. Remains of these paintings are found on the Pajarito Plateau in New Mexico and in the Jeddito area. There are numerous Spanish accounts of house and kiva painting in villages they visited in the sixteenth century. During the Awatovi Expedition kiva murals were found at Awatovi and Kawaika-a, apparently first appearing during the late 1300s.

This sudden artistic vitality is also reflected in the manufacture of pottery. During the middle part of the fourteenth century, yellow pottery replaced the white, gray and red pottery of the previous 500 years. The appearance of a yellow pottery closely corresponds to the use of coal in the firing of pottery and this may explain its sudden appearance (Bartlett 1935:44). This pottery maintains the same geometric designs of its predecessors until the late 1300s. By 1400 the pottery type known as Sikyatki Polychrome was being manufactured (fig. 3). The painted designs on this pottery are strongly reminiscent of the kiva murals (Smith 1952:149).

*On the walls of the rooms where we were quartered were many paintings of the demons they worship as gods. Fierce and terrible were their features.*

Gaspar Pérez de Villagrá, 1610
*History of New Mexico* translated by Gilberto Espinosa, 1933.

Fig. 3. Sikyatki Polychrome, 1375-1630. Photographed by Mark Middleton. Courtesy of the Museum of Northern Arizona.

# The Kachina Cult

During the fourteenth century basic changes or additions to the already established cultural pattern occurred over a broad area in these early Pueblo IV villages. This elaboration of culture is most strikingly manifested in the pottery and in the murals (Smith 1952). This change in artistic expression undoubtedly reflected a change in world view. The preceding ceramic and mural painting traditions emphasized simple, symmetrical, repetitive geometric forms. The new tradition utilized asymmetrical, complex, curvilinear designs, abstract designs, and realistic designs depicting a variety of life forms. Within the mural panels masked beings strongly reminiscent of modern and historic kachinas are portrayed. This suggests that the kachina cult was associated with this complex of traits and that the kachina society was accepted at this time (ca. 1350-1400) by numerous, widespread villages from the Zuñi area to the Little Colorado River Valley and the Hopi mesas. With the addition of the kachina cult trait complex, indigenous people bearing this culture can be identified as Hopi or Zuñi.

It is interesting to speculate on the origins of this cult, or religious society, and the reason for its rapid and widespread acceptance by the local populace. Its origins are not an issue for this paper except to note that Hopi mythology and present archaeological data point to the south or southeast. The twelfth century Mimbres ceramic tradition in southwestern New Mexico certainly resembles the vitality and general representationalism of the fourteenth century trait complex, as does the ceramic tradition at Casas Grandes in northeastern Mexico dating to the twelfth and thirteenth centuries (DiPeso 1974: 531-539, volume 6). Petroglyphs from the vicinity of El Paso apparently depict masked beings (kachinas?) dating to ca. A.D. 1150 (Dockstader 1954:35; Schaafsma and Schaafsma 1974: 537-538). Perhaps these, too, are part of a larger interaction sphere for this kachina cult trait complex.

But why were the kachina cult and related traits so readily assimilated by the local populace? It surely must relate to a primary function of the modern Hopi kachina society, which is the bringing of moisture. Note the word moisture. A long-term drought, such as that in the late thirteenth century, affects the environment for many years afterward (Eddy 1972:6-14; Dean 1969:12-13; Bradfield 1971:28-29). Reduction of the local vegetational cover promotes runoff, and results in arroyo cutting (Dean 1969:12-13; Bradfield 1971:28-29). Thus, the effects on local vegetation and crops would surely long outlive the actual drought. Compare the modern Hopi and the effects of arroyo cutting on their economy 75 years after the event (Bradfield 1971:28-29) where most of the agricultural areas in the valleys have been abandoned in favor of akchin, sand dune or spring-fed agricultural plots. The inhabitants of northeastern Arizona in the second half of the fourteenth century were probably still feeling the effects of the drought and associated environmental chaos of the previous 100 years. Into this stress situation a new cult, such as the kachina society which focused on environmental "control," would be welcomed and readily assimilated.

To support a growing population, as demonstrated historically, more than dry farming would be necessary. Springs are abundant, both along the mesas and in the washes and could be controlled for irrigation. There are water-control systems in the vicinity of the large sites. All of these require substantial cooperation from an entire village. This does not necessarily require a centralized authority but it does require an organization at least as powerful as historic, traditional Hopi villages, where the "chief" of the village owns all of the village land and theoretically could control its use and productivity.

It is the feeling of the author that this central authority may be a vestige of a more powerful central authority in the fifteenth century. This political system ties directly with the appearance of the kachina cult. One primary function of the kachina in modern Hopi society is association with the redistribution of food both in the kiva and in households. Both the central authority and redistribution are indicative of some social stratification in Hopi society and the development of incipient chiefdoms. Perhaps craft specialization was also associated with this trait complex to which the florescence of the arts can be attributed (Sahlins 1974:170-177).

It seems likely that this authority was tied to necessity. Because this new mode of social organization was adaptive, it was accepted. Even today one is struck by the adaptiveness of Hopi culture. When the stress causing this adaptive strategy relaxed, so did the social system tied to it, and as a result the more centralized aspects of Hopi society are no longer operative.

# The Period 1540-1870

This social system was soon disrupted permanently with early Spanish contact. The first contact by Pedro de Tobar and Juan de Padilla, who were dispatched from Zuñi by Coronado, occurred in 1540. Early contact was sporadic and had little or no effect on the Hopi until the establishment of the first mission at Awatovi in 1629. The only result from this early Spanish contact was small-scale trading which may have resulted in the Hopi acquisition of some domesticated plants and animals and bartering for a few material items. In 1629 there were only five or six Hopi villages with a population of about 3000, evidently a considerable decline from the fifteenth century population.

The purpose of the mission program from 1629 to 1680 was *directed cultural change*. The geographic isolation of the Hopi helped to ameliorate the effects of the Spanish program. The logistics involved, plus the constant bickering between church and state, made the Spaniards' impact on Hopi social, political and religious systems a minor one. However, economically there were long-lasting effects. The Spaniards introduced numerous domesticated animals and plants of which all but wheat are still used today. The purpose of these introductions by the Spaniards

Fig. 4. (L) San Bernardo Polychrome, 1630-1680. (R) Payupki Polychrome, 1680-1820. Photographed by Mark Middleton. Courtesy of the Museum of Northern Arizona.

was to promote the economic self-sufficiency of each mission village. Other introductions were weaving with wool, blacksmithing, farming implements, and smallpox.

The 1680 Pueblo Revolt effectively ended the Spanish period at Hopi, though there was an abortive attempt to reestablish a mission at Awatovi in 1700. Following the revolt, the Spaniards, through Governor de Vargas, reestablished control in all Pueblo villages except Hopi by 1692. Subsequently, additional revolts occurred in New Mexico in 1693 and 1696. The result of these revolts and subsequent Spanish repression was an exodus of New Mexico Pueblo people seeking refuge in the Hopi villages.

Shortly after 1690 the people of Walpi, Shongopavi (*Songoopavi*) and Mishongnovi (*Musangnuvi*) moved from the bases of their respective mesas to the mesa tops in anticipation of Spanish reprisals for their participation in the revolt and for harboring the New Mexico refugees. Much of the discussion which follows, dealing with specific changes in material culture, is derived from excavations by the Museum of Northern Arizona at Walpi from 1975 to 1977.

The result of these events was the swelling of the local population—a population composed of the apostates of frontier New Spain. Strong anti-Spaniard feeling was harbored among these unlikely allies, a feeling which cemented their alliance for 50 years. The effect of this anti-Spaniard feeling is noticeable in the material remains at Walpi.

During the mission period Hopi ceramics reflected Spanish contact in form as well as design. The broad, flaring rimmed stew or bread bowls and the base ring on many vessel forms identify the Hopi-made mission ware of this period (fig. 4L). Arabesque, spiral volute, and other design motifs indicative of Spanish influence also became common. After the revolt all elements of form or design reminiscent of the Spanish disappeared. These omissions can best be explained as a symbolic rejection of Spanish culture.

Post-1690 bowl and jar forms and design motifs resemble contemporary Tewa and Keres pottery, e.g., Ogapoge, Puname and Tewa Polychrome made in the Rio Grande Valley (figs. 3 & 4R; cf. Frank and Harlow 1974).

Introductions by the Spaniards of more useful items, such as wool in textiles and domesticated plants and animals, were retained. Thus by the middle of the eighteenth century, cotton had been almost completely replaced by wool, and sheep and goat had replaced antelope as primary meat sources. Clearly, the apostate allies were selective in their rejection of all Spanish introductions.

During the 1730s a series of dry years made food supplies uncomfortably short. This shortage, plus the lack of a strong enemy against whom the Hopi could unite, served to weaken their alliance, resulting in infighting (Brew 1949:32). As a result, beginning in 1742, the refugees began returning home. By 1780 all but the inhabitants of Hano (*Haano*), a Tewa village still inhabited on First Mesa, had returned to their homeland. Concomitant with these events, anti-Spaniard feeling among the Hopi declined. After 1750 Spanish elements reappear on Hopi pottery, though the form and overall design motifs remained Tewan.

From 1777 to 1780 a severe drought struck Hopi country followed by a smallpox epidemic in 1781 (Spicer 1967:195). These disasters prompted many Hopi families to abandon their homes and move to Zuñi, Acoma, Zia, Sandia and other pueblos where they had friends or relatives. Upon the return of the rains and the people, a striking change in ceramics is noted. The unslipped tan or orange pottery with Tewa designs of the preceding period was replaced with a white slipped vessel with modified Tewa elements. Spanish forms, such as stew bowls, again became popular and design elements borrowed from the Spaniards reappear (fig. 5L). These intrusions of Spanish culture into Hopi were assimilated indirectly through their acculturated Pueblo relatives and friends. These effects were probably also noticeable in the ceremonial sphere of Hopi culture. Numerous elements of Spanish culture such as the use of bells for rattles, the belief that any individual can be a witch, and the shifting of the kachina calendar to coincide with many Catholic saints' days (Parsons 1939:1064-1084) can be traced in Pueblo religion (Dockstader 1954:73).

Beginning about 1780, intensifying ca. 1810 and continuing to 1863, Navajo aids presented a disruptive influence on Hopi society. This disruption amounted to no more than the destruction of a few fields or the theft of livestock; however, frequently it resulted in loss of life. In 1837 the entire village of Oraibi was forced to scatter before a Navajo raid (Spicer 1967: 213). The effects of these raids are still visible today at Walpi. The ruins of stock pens built against the mesa edge to protect livestock at night are still visible. The Hopi sought relief from these raids through the Spanish Government in 1819 and the United States Government in 1857, but received no relief until the Kit Carson campaign resulted in Navajo subjugation at Fort Sumner in 1863-1864.

In 1853 a severe smallpox epidemic struck First Mesa reducing the population from 1200 to 650 by 1861 (Bradfield 1971: 61). At Walpi, the population was reduced from over 500 to less than 300. Archaeologically, we can detect the effects of this epidemic with the abandonment of parts of the village. Numerous inhabitants again left their homes for those of friends at Zuñi and Acoma and the ceramic remains reflect this with more change. In fact archaeological evidence reveals a continuous, substantial contact between the Zuñi and the Hopi beginning about the time of persistent, intensive Navajo raiding. It is conceivable that during times of peace (lulls in raiding) the Navajo served as traders between the villages (Forbes 1960:238). Ceramically, this contact with Zuñi is most visible; however, basketry and other remains also reveal a strong, continuous flow and interchange of material goods and probably ideas.

Fig. 5. (L) Early Polacca Polychrome, 1780-1850. (R) Late Polacca Polychrome, 1865-1910. Photographed by Mark Middleton. Courtesy of the Museum of Northern Arizona.

The severe depopulation of Walpi also may have disrupted the social and religious systems of the Hopi. It was apparently at this time that the Bear Clan became extinct at Walpi (Eggan 1950:64). Since this clan was the ruling clan of the village from which the village chief was chosen, the political and social systems were affected. Perhaps most important, the religious functions of the clan were either lost or taken over by another clan or clans. The ramifications for the present-day First Mesa religious system are worthy of a detailed analysis.

In times of stress the Hopi sought refuge with the Zuñi. This occurred in the 1770s, in 1853, and again from 1864 to 1868 when another devastating drought struck the Hopi (Spicer 1967: 201). Historic documents report the virtual abandonment of Hopi. Upon their return the people were making pottery which, except for its orange or yellow paste, was identical to contemporary Zuñi pottery (fig.5R). Also, as noted by Spicer (1967:201), new elements were introduced into the ceremonial cycle of the Hopi. On First Mesa these may have served as a replacement of those lost or disrupted with the extinction of the Bear Clan. The curing elements in First Mesa ceremonialism may also have been introduced at this time in response to the 1853 epidemic.

# The Period 1870 to the Present

Primary contacts of the Hopi with Euro-American culture from 1870 to 1910 came through the presence of federal government representatives and traders. These two groups were major factors in the material culture change of the Hopi.

Special Indian agents began visiting the Hopi by 1870. A practice of the American government was the distribution of tools and farming implements to the heads of households. In the 1870s the types of goods distributed included camp kettles, axes, pickaxes, spades and garden seeds (Palmer 1870:596). Also at this time, plows and cultivators were given to the Hopi men but they were not used, since the Hopi had neither horses nor harness trappings (Donaldson 1893:43). By the 1880s the then annual distribution of goods included clothing, wagons, harness, cook stoves and farm tools (Bowman 1884:138; Patterson 1887:178; Patterson 1888:196). The practice of giving away goods was replaced in 1910 by the exchange of goods for labor.

The material culture of the Hopi was further altered by the influence of the government schools on the children. When the first government-operated boarding school was opened in 1887, children were brought to school by their parents or were sometimes forcibly taken from their homes by government school workers (Udall 1969:8; Dockstader 1954:84). In exchange for bringing their children to school, fathers were given axes, hammers and lamps, and mothers were given dress cloth (Simmons 1942:94). At school the children's native clothes were taken away and replaced with shirts, shoes and khaki pants or overalls for the boys and dresses, petticoats, shoes and aprons for the girls

(Udall 1969:92; Simmons 1942:90; Neville 1952:45). After their time at school many children continued wearing their American-style clothes. The boarding school removed the children from their homes for extended periods. The goal of this system was to completely break the traditional patterns of the Indians and assimilate them into the white community (McIntire: 1968:75). One boarding school and four day schools were on the Hopi reservation by 1910.

With the intrusion of Euro-American culture into Hopi life, a period of crisis appeared on the Hopi Reservation. Euro-American culture by the 1880s and 1890s represented the same attempt at directed culture change as posed by the Spaniards 250 years earlier. These intrusions were symbolized through government efforts to educate their children, missionary attempts to convert them and trade goods to replace traditional material culture. Hopi resistance, similar to post-Pueblo Revolt period, may have been symbolized by a return to traditional ceramic values. The Sikyatki revival ware (also called Hano Polychrome) attributed to Nampeyo (fig. 6) may be one manifestation of this feeling.

Another symbol of this revolt resulted in the split at Oraibi in 1906. As early as 1871 there were two factions at Oraibi, pro-government and antigovernment. The antigovernment faction refused a census in 1871. Numerous incidents served to widen the schism, such as the forcible placement of children in schools by the government from 1890 to 1894, the attempt to subject the Hopi to a land allotment program, and the interference of the Mennonite church in village affairs beginning in the early 1890s. By 1896 the two sides were holding separate ceremonies. In 1906 the leader of the antigovernment faction challenged the progovernment faction to a pushing match, the loser to leave the

Fig. 6. Hano Polychrome, 1885-present. Nampeyo. H: 13.5 cm. Dia: 34 cm. California Academy of Sciences, Elkus Collection 370-165.

Fig. 7. Hopi children at Polacca Sunday School. Photographed by Joseph Mora, 1905. Courtesy of John R. Wilson.

Fig. 8. Jack Walker's Trading Post at Talchaco, Arizona, on the Little Colorado River. Photographed by Joseph Mora, 1904-1906. Courtesy of John R. Wilson.

village. The antigovernment faction lost, left Oraibi, and founded the village of Hotevilla (Ho'atvela).

The trading posts were also a major factor leading to change in the material culture. The first trading post was established in 1875 and was located approximately twelve miles from Walpi. By 1910 seven traders were located on the reservation—four Hopi and three licensed white traders (Miller 1910:4). The trading posts carried only general merchandise; no patent medicines of any kind were sold. The posts dealt mostly in necessity items such as canned foods, coffee, hardware, cloth and other staple products for which the Hopi bartered. By the late 1890s they realized it was easier to get cloth from traders than weave it themselves (Donaldson 1893:46). Men bought unbleached muslin from the trading posts and sewed their own trousers and shirts. Women obtained gingham or calico which they used in the same manner as the traditional manta or women's dress. Young girls, having felt the influence of the government schools, sewed the store-bought cotton cloth into dresses (Udall 1969:49).

By the late 1880s Euro-American cultural influence could be seen in Hopi homes. Some American furniture was beginning to be used and glass began to replace selenite windowpanes (Bourke 1884:115; Means 1960:53). Kerosene lamps also became more common because of their convenience. Hopi architecture was altered. In particular, doors in side walls began to replace roof entrances (Means 1960:53).

The Walpi artifactual material indicates the great importance the Hopi placed on the tools given to them by the government. Axes are one of the most numerous artifacts found. It was noted in the 1890s that iron and steel tools were rapidly replacing the stone tools traditionally used (Bourke 1884:25). Metal artifacts, mostly hardware items, rather than glass or ceramic remains, are the most common items found at Walpi prior to 1910. The lack of knives, forks and other tableware items suggests that at Walpi they were not used to any great extent before 1910. Glass trade beads came into prominence at Walpi during this second period and it is probable that the Hopi were acquiring them from the trading posts.

The material culture of the Hopi was altered substantially during the time period 1870 to 1910. In 1870 the American culture had barely affected the Hopi. Forty years later the Hopi were wearing American clothes, using steel and iron tools and bartering for staple food products—reflecting the influence of the trading post and the American Government.

Beginning around 1910, new villages, such as Polacca below First Mesa and Kyakotsmovi (Kiqötsmovi) below Third Mesa, were founded at the bases of the mesas for various economic, social and political reasons (Eggan 1950:134). The valley villages became the focus for American influences such as missions, schools and trading posts (Spicer 1962:205). The years 1910 through 1943 are also the time of increasing conflict between the Navajo and the Hopi over the borders between their reservations. This dispute was temporarily settled in 1943 when the U.S. Government gave three-fourths of the Hopi reservation established in 1882 to the Navajo.

On July 22, 1958, Congress passed an act which convened a three judge court to settle the dispute which the 1943 program was supposed to settle. In the decision ( Healing vs. Jones 1962) of this court, Land District No. 6 was given exclusively to the Hopi Tribe, and the Hopi and Navajo hold joint, undivided, and equal interest to the balance of the 1882 reservation. Today this is referred to as the joint use area. The Hopi-Navajo Settlement Act of 1974 authorized the court to partition the land. In February 1977, a land dispute decision was rendered in which the joint use area was divided equally between the Hopi and the Navajo. The decision based the boundaries of the division on what would minimally dislocate people. As a result, the western and southern sections of the joint use area go to the Hopi and the northern and eastern sections go to the Navajo. An island of Navajo land is established within the Hopi land east of Keams Canyon, which is referred to as the Jeddito Island. The Hopi also have an island of land surrounded by Navajo land to the west of the mesas around the town of Moenkopi (Munqapi). This decision is being disputed by the Navajo and many issues are yet to be resolved.

By 1913, 30 percent of the Hopi were dressing like the white man, and by 1943 traditional clothing was worn only for ceremonies (Crane 1913:5). The move off the mesas made the use of

Fig. 9. Hano, First Mesa. Photographed by Joseph Mora, 1904-1906. Courtesy of John R. Wilson.

Fig. 10. Walpi potter wearing Anglo calico dress, First Mesa. Photographed by E. B. Sayles, 1930-1940. Courtesy of the Arizona State Museum, University of Arizona.

wagons more practical and convenient, and as a result, an increasing number of Hopi began to use them. The more prosperous Hopi, such as the traders, were able to afford automobiles, although these did not come into common use before 1940. Only a few Hopi were using plows and cultivators by 1911; however, by 1943 their use was widespread (Lawshe 1911:14). The effect of the trading post on the economy continued to increase during the 1920s, when it became common for the men to buy their shirts, pants and shoes there. Women, however, tended to sew their own clothes rather than purchase them from the trading post (Neville 1952:45). Inventories from the trading posts show that a greater variety of goods were becoming available to the Hopi. The Walpi material suggests that canned goods, especially baking powder and vegetables, were being acquired from

the posts. The inventories also list a number of new luxury items such as perfumes and soaps, as well as new appliances and improvements for the home such as sewing machines and sadirons.

By 1930, 85 percent of the Hopi were speaking and reading English (McIntire 1968:76). This facilitated the use of mail-order catalogues by the Hopi. Various page fragments from Sears' and Ward's catalogues found at the excavations at Walpi indicate that the people were ordering from the catalogues by the 1930s. The Walpi material also shows that magazines had become available by this time and the schools were providing the children with books and magazines, such as "The Weekly Reader."

Artifactual material from Walpi suggests that stoves as well as a number of kitchen utensils, such as spoons, pans and coffee pots, were used in homes during the 1920s and 1930s. Ceramic dishes, plates and cups were also in use, as were metal knives, forks and spoons. The influence of Euro-American material culture on the Hopi is also noticeable through the increased use of window glass and the covering of dirt floors with linoleum.

During the years 1943 to the present the Hopi embraced nearly all aspects of the Euro-American material culture. It is also a time when the Hopi changed from a subsistence economy

Fig. 11. Interior of Charles Frederick's piki house. Note the juxtaposition of Anglo wax paper, coffee cans and metal buckets with the traditional piki bowl, tray and stone. Courtesy of the Museum of Northern Arizona E124/3358.l.

Fig. 12. Children playing at Second Mesa. Photographed by Hans Halberstadt, 1979. Courtesy of the California Academy of Sciences.

supplemented by cash and trade goods to a cash economy supplemented by the persistence of a traditional subsistence economy (Kennard 1965:25). World War II and the stock reduction program of 1943 were two factors that led to this change.

World War II brought many changes to Hopi life. Several hundred men left the reservation to join the armed forces. Other men and women also left the reservation to work as industrial workers in nearby towns and cities (Thompson 1950:40). After the war many Hopi did not return to the reservation but instead sought employment in towns adjacent to it (Kennard 1965:26).

In 1943 the stock reduction program greatly reduced the number of livestock on the reservation. This program forced returning veterans out of a subsistence based on raising livestock into earning the salary and wages, often off the reservation, offered by the American cash economy (Adams 1978:51).

The move off the reservation placed the Hopi in greater contact with the white culture, and the change to a cash economy allowed the Hopi to purchase greater amounts of Euro-American goods. The Hopi were provided better access to nearby towns when roads were paved in the 1950s and 1960s connecting the reservation to the outside world and encouraging the widespread use of automobiles. The trading posts and mail-order catalogues continued to supply the Indians on the reservation with the majority of their goods in the 1940s. However, by the 1950s the trading posts were losing a great deal of trade (Kennard 1965:28), since the Hopi were making increased use of the stores in the nearby cities of Holbrook, Winslow and Flagstaff, which provided them with a greater variety of items.

The Walpi artifactual material reflects the increased purchasing of Euro-American goods by the Hopi following World War II. Many types of manufactured clothes, tools and toys were found. Especially abundant was plastic material, including toys, hair accessories and personal ornaments. Plastic cups, plates, spoons and forks were also common.

Manufactured clothing has been used predominantly by the Hopi since the 1940s. Work shirts, denim jeans and work boots were the common garb of the men for field work. Cowboy boots and hats were common by the 1950s. The Hopi women characteristically wore cotton dresses and tennis shoes (Neville 1952: 52). The trading posts and mail-order catalogues probably supplied the Hopi with most of their clothing during the 1940s and part of the 1950s, but by the late 1950s the Hopi began purchasing most of their clothing at the city stores.

The artifactual material from Walpi also indicates that processed foods were making their way into Hopi homes by the 1940s. Cracker Jack box wrappers were the most common evidence of the white man's influence. The presence of Cracker Jack also accounts for the number of plastic toys (prizes) found. Other evidences of processed foods include bread wrappers, candy wrappers, peanut butter jars and pickle jars. Soda pop became popular around the 1940s, and pop bottles accounted for much of the glass remains found at Walpi. Reading materials, dating after 1940, were unearthed at Walpi, including magazines, newspapers and books. Trading posts were carrying magazines and books by the 1940s but did not have a great variety from which to choose. It is probable that most of the reading material was obtained from city stores. Children's schoolbooks were also found, as were a number of religious magazines written for a young audience.

# Conclusions

The Hopi have resisted, sometimes violently, culture change, especially directed culture change as imposed by Spanish culture and Euro-American culture. However, if allowed to assimilate the foreign culture, change progresses relatively smoothly and rapidly. Today, Hopi culture is an amalgamation of Euro-American culture and traditional Hopi culture. The result is a culture quite different from the traditional one, one hundred years ago, but one which certainly is not Euro-American.

The ability of the Hopi to change, aided by the retention of their original land base, traditional homes and religious beliefs, has provided the key to the continuity of their culture. Whether adaptability can keep pace with change to ensure this continuity, especially with the decline of native religion, is a question only the future can answer.

E. Charles Adams
*Principal Investigator, Walpi Archaeological Project*
*Museum of Northern Arizona*

Deborah Hull
*Assistant, Walpi Archaeological Project*
*Museum of Northern Arizona*

# MURAL DECORATIONS FROM ANCIENT HOPI KIVAS

Fig. 13. Sikyatki mural, Awatovi, Test 14, Room 3
Front B Design No. 11. All photographs courtesy of
Watson Smith.

# by Watson Smith

Although the Hopi today occupy several clusters of villages from First Mesa in the east to Moenkopi (*Munqapi*) in the west, in the late prehistoric period their territory extended farther eastward for about twenty-five kilometers. The major topographic feature of this wider area is Antelope Mesa, below which flows the intermittent Jeddito Wash. Above the steep escarpment of Antelope Mesa were situated at least five large pueblos and several smaller villages, most of them occupied probably into the fourteenth century. Two of them, Awatovi and Kawaika-a, were occupied well into the sixteenth century.

The first contact between indigenous peoples of the American Southwest and Europeans occurred in A.D. 1540 with the arrival of Francisco Vásquez de Coronado at the Zuñi pueblo of Háwikuh. Coronado dispatched a small party, under the command of Don García López de Cárdenas, to explore the unknown country northwest of Zuñi. After a few days' travel Cárdenas came upon a pueblo village which he does not name, but which must have been either Awatovi or Kawaika-a. This meeting apparently did not greatly affect the Hopi, since Cárdenas' most famous accomplishment of this trip was being the first European to discover the Grand Canyon of the Colorado.

For nearly a century afterwards no significant results followed upon this fateful meeting, but in A.D. 1630 a campaign of religious conversion was mounted by the Spanish Franciscan Order based in Santa Fe, and several missions were established in the Hopi villages. Apparently by this time Kawaika-a had been deserted by its populace, but Awatovi, the largest of the Hopi towns, still flourished. Here the friars built their major church and convento and remained in precarious control for fifty years until 1680, when the resident Spaniards were killed and the church was razed during the Pueblo Revolt. An abortive attempt at reoccupation was made by the Spanish in 1699 but with only momentary success. The entire village was soon destroyed, and its people were killed or carried away by noncollaborating Hopi from other villages in 1700.

Since this time, Awatovi lay in stately if ruinous peace for two centuries until archaeologists first dug their questing spades into its soil in the 1890s. In 1935 the Peabody Museum of Harvard University, under the direction of J. O. Brew, began a five-year exploration of Awatovi from its unknown beginnings through

*During the night a forbidding-looking party of strangers had quietly made camp under the protection of the cliffs. The sharp eyes of the Hopi saw men with bearded faces that were white. But stranger still, these curious white-faced men had with them great animals such as no Hopi had ever seen or heard of. Were they some species of monstrous dog?*

*As they watched, these beasts occasionally pawed the ground and snorted, blowing puffs of smoke—or was it simply dust?—into the air. A few of these creatures were even more fearsome to behold—they seemed part man and part animal, for the upper part of a white man's body grew up from their backs. There were gasps of astonishment when one of these hybrid animals began to split in two, and the man-like part of it suddenly displayed legs and jumped to the ground where it walked about like any other man.*

Harry C. James
*Pages from Hopi History*

the period of Spanish dominance.

Inference from historic pueblo practices and from the actual excavation by Dr. Walter Hough in 1901 of a painted fragment in a kiva at Kawaika-a prepared archaeologists for the exciting discovery of a kiva at Awatovi with painted walls dating from about the early fifteenth century. Subsequent investigation at both Awatovi and Kawaika-a uncovered the remains of more than 200 individual paintings on the walls of about twenty kivas. Many more wall paintings undoubtedly remain undiscovered in these and other ancient Hopi villages.

Kiva walls at Awatovi were then, as now, constructed of roughly coursed sandstone blocks, which were chinked and crudely finished with coatings of coarse mud mortar. Over these were applied thin layers about 1.25 mm in thickness of finish plaster composed of fine homogeneous reddish-brown sandy clay. These coats were renewed from time to time, and in one instance more than 100 superimposed coats, with a total thickness of about 11 cm, had survived on a single wall.

On these finish coats were painted elaborate designs in a variety of colors. Pigments were mostly minerals readily available in the vicinity, producing various shades of yellow, orange and red, all from iron oxides; pink and vermilion from mixtures of red ochre and white or gray clays; brown from red ochre mixed with fine particles of charcoal; maroon from red ochre combined with a mineral containing manganese; blue, occasionally from azurite, but much more commonly from a mixture of charcoal and white clay, which surprisingly gave the optical effect of dull gray-blue; green, which was rare, from malachite or sometimes from yellow iron oxide mixed with charcoal. White was derived from relatively pure kaolin; black (the only organic pigment present) was charcoal or bone black.

The vehicle with which the pigments were mixed was probably a vegetable or animal oil mixed with water or saliva. The paints were evidently applied with a stiff brush, such as the frayed end of a yucca leaf, but sometimes with the fingers, as was evident from occasional fingerprints.

It is not possible here to discuss the vast and intricate subject of Pueblo ceremonialism, but it may be said that today most Pueblo ceremonials are conducted in kivas by the members of certain societies. Usually these ceremonials are of several days' duration, and special preparations are made for each one, including sand paintings on the floor, vertical altars with a wide variety of sacred and symbolic objects, and, sometimes ceremonial paintings upon kiva walls. After the conclusion of a particular ceremonial the accoutrements are removed and stored in secrecy, and the mural paintings are obliterated by being washed from the walls.

By analogy to observed and recorded ethnographic examples, it is reasonable to infer that similar procedures were followed in ancient times, except for one very important difference. During the occupation of the Antelope Mesa villages, the kiva wall paintings were covered but not destroyed after the conclusion of a particular ceremonial, by being sealed behind a new coating of sandy-clay plaster. The wall then became available for the application of a new painting appropriate for a subsequent ceremony. This replastering procedure brought a fortuitous reward, since it provided the means for permanent preservation of a graphic record that would otherwise have disappeared forever.

However, the task of exposing, copying and removing these treasures was exceedingly difficult. Since there was no exact precedent for working with kiva murals, the task had to be approached pragmatically. It was found that in almost all instances higher portions of the walls had collapsed, leaving an irregular broken edge along the plaster layers. Furthermore, in many cases, the plaster had broken away from the wall behind it and was sustained only by the pressure of the debris that filled the room. The removal of this debris therefore risked the collapse of the plaster integument. By trial and error a simple expedient was worked out for supporting the standing plaster layers by patching and sealing them with a mortar of the very same sandy clay of which the original layers had been composed, and sometimes by erecting a temporary framework set snugly against the plaster face and anchored in the floor. It was then easy to photograph and copy the outermost painting (fig. 14). All details were sketched to scale with the aid of a grid laid over the original, descriptive notes were made and samples taken of all color variations of the paint.

The most delicate problem was how to expose the next underlying layer without damaging it and without sacrificing the outermost layer. Fortunately the painting technique used was not true fresco, a technique whereby paint is applied to still damp plaster, which absorbs the paint as it dries. Instead, the paint was applied on dry plaster in a manner called *fresco secco*. In this technique the paint forms a thin film with only a superficial bond to the underlying plaster.

The benevolent kachinas (*katsinam*) must have been watching over the puzzled archaeologists at Awatovi, for at exactly this time an identical situation had been discovered at the contemporary Pueblo ruin of Kuaua near Bernalillo, New Mexico. At Kuaua a single kiva had disclosed a wall that bore multiple layers of paintings. By herculean efforts this entire wall was jacketed in a reinforced plaster cocoon and transported to the University of New Mexico in Albuquerque, where a process for the stripping of the successive layers was being developed by Dr. Gordon Vivian, Mr. Wesley Bliss and others. Through their generous collaboration, a similar procedure was adopted at Awatovi, although there the stripping had to be done in the field, with exposure to the uncooperative elements of wind, sun and rain, since the removal of entire walls to a sheltered laboratory was not feasible.

The stripping was accomplished by applying an acetone-soluble synthetic adhesive to the painted surface and covering

Fig. 14. Awatovi, Room 788, Left Wall, Design 8, Watson Smith making drawing of mural.

Fig. 15. Applying adhesive to mural.

this still tacky surface with a sheet of thin muslin (fig. 15). When thoroughly dry the muslin could be peeled from the surface, just as adhesive tape can be removed from the skin, bringing with it the film of paint, which would separate cleanly from its underlying plaster.

It is hardly necessary to say that under field conditions many of the requirements were difficult to achieve: the adhesive had to be spread evenly; it had to dry rapidly but not too rapidly; it had to be sufficiently viscous to prevent penetration of the pores within the sandy plaster; it had to resist absorption of moisture from the atmosphere or from the plaster itself; the muslin had to be cut and applied in squares of a size that was manageable under windy conditions; and of course the weather had to be propitious (fig. 16). Under optimum conditions the result was a film of paint adhering face down against a supporting fabric of adhesive and muslin, which could then be stripped from the wall, rolled like wallpaper and taken to the Peabody Museum in Cambridge for remounting (fig. 17).

Having successfully stripped a painted layer, it was then necessary to remove the underlying and now sterile plaster in order to expose the next painted layer behind it. This was done by means of that technological workhorse, the Boy Scout knife, which had to be neither too sharp nor too dull, so that the granular plaster could be gently abraded and separated from the paint beneath it. Then for each successive painted layer the procedure began all over again, until the bottom and earliest layer had been recovered.

In Cambridge the stripped painting was mounted on a permanent backing for preservation and display. In some cases the stripping was mounted directly on tempered Masonite, which provided a fairly close match for the color of the original plaster. In other instances a thin coating of plaster composed of the actual sandy clay of the originals was spread upon the Masonite and the stripped section was mounted thereon.

To accomplish this the surface of the permanent support was coated with an adhesive different from that used in the field, and upon this the muslin sheet was spread so that the reverse of the original paint film adhered to the new support. The original adhesive was then dissolved in acetone, thus freeing the muslin sheet from the paint film, and it could then be removed, exposing the remounted painting safely supported by its new backing. The success of this operation required that the final mounting adhesive be insoluble in acetone—otherwise it would be removed with the muslin.

In this instance a water-soluble animal-derived glue was used, but one potential problem with animal-derived glues is that fungus will attack and ultimately destroy the glue. However, addition of a chemical fungicide to the adhesive solution during its preparation will suppress fungus growth. It is gratifying that forty years later the remounted specimens show no evidence of deterioration.

In practice not all of the more than 200 paintings or fragments thereof were actually stripped and remounted. Since this was a tedious task and time was a vital factor in the field, a hard decision had to be made between the competing ideal of com-

Fig. 16. Applying muslin to mural.

Fig. 17. Stripping muslin with painting from wall.

plete preservation of all paintings and that of uncovering and recording as many different examples as possible. Only those most nearly complete or most spectacular and interesting in detail were preserved intact. All others were carefully copied in scale drawings amplified by photographs, notes and paint samples, and these were later reproduced at the museum. The reproductions were done at half scale on heavy illustration board, the surface of which was prepared by a flocking process, whereby a liquid of glue sizing containing a reddish-brown pigment was sprayed on the board in such a manner as to produce a fine granular surface that closely resembled the texture and color of the original wall plaster. On this surface an exact rendering of the painting was then executed in opaque watercolor, using the field sketches, notes, paint samples and photographs as basic data.

The artistry and craftsmanship of the ancient Hopi mural paintings are of several styles, which show changes over the centuries from comparatively simple geometric, almost abstract beginnings to detailed representational compositions portraying the personages, animals and paraphernalia involved in particular ceremonies. The execution, while precise and balanced, was usually static, sometimes almost like the frozen instant of a single frame in a moving picture.

However, a few of the later compositions possess a more fluid style in which the feeling of movement was more effectively achieved. Several of the latter portrayed scenes of symbolic combat between two anthropomorphic figures, some of which can, with a degree of certainty, be identified as representing actions that are still today carried out in certain ceremonials.

Both styles contained essentially the same elements, principally kachinas and human figures; a wide assortment of plants, such as corn, beans, squash and cactus; animals, including badgers, rabbits, deer, snakes, lizards, birds, fish and frogs; pahos (*paavaho*), tiponis (*tiitiponi*), crooks, feathers, animal skins, bows, arrows, shields, clouds, lightning and other features symbolic of the purposes and requirements of a particular religious observance. It seems quite clear that paintings of this kind were mimetic of the living scene that was acted out either in the kiva or at an associated dance in the village plaza.

Among the best-preserved mural paintings at Awatovi were those from a kiva designated Room 788, which was found directly beneath the sanctuary of the Franciscan church. As was often their practice, the Spanish fathers had purposely positioned their most sacred structure over an existing shrine of the Indians as a visual symbol of the supplanting of the old faith by the new. The kiva was deliberately filled with clean sand, and its roof and walls were left intact, so that the paintings had suffered much less deterioration than had those in other kivas. An example is shown in (Color Plate 8).

While the representational style became more intricate during later years, geometric and abstract compositions never died out. Some of the most complex and involved patterns occurred

Fig. 18. Awatovi, Test 14, Room 3, Front B Wall, Design No. 2.

Fig. 19. Awatovi, Room 788, Left Wall, Design No. 3.

Fig. 20. Awatovi, Room 529, Right Wall, Design 1 (right ½).

contemporaneously with explicitly representational scenes and were the most beautiful and carefully planned of all. Several of these were designed and executed in the convoluted manner of the Sikyatki style of decoration that appeared on certain pottery vessels current in the late sixteenth century, which were probably the most elaborate and beautiful ceramic achievement of the prehistoric Pueblo peoples. An outstanding example is shown in figure 13.

The name is derived from the discovery of many examples at the excavation of the ruined pueblo of Sikyatki, just east of First Mesa, by J. W. Fewkes in the late nineteenth century. Nothing comparable to them had been made for almost four centuries until a well-known potter named Nampeyo, then living in the village of Hano (Haano) on First Mesa, inspired by these ancient designs, created a revised version of the old Sikyatki style, adapted and modified by her own genius. This tradition has been carried on by several of Nampeyo's descendants and other recent potters and has come to be known by her name.

Although these designs appear at first glance to be entirely geometric, they were in fact composed of many abstract renderings of elements from Nature: birds' feathers and tails, mythical beasts, cloud forms, stars, lightning, growing plants, water symbols, prayer plumes, tiponis and the like.

In some cases portrayals in particular paintings can be equated with personages in modern ceremonies. An example is shown in figure 18, which depicts a combat between costumed antagonists. This may be a rendering of the symbolic combat that occurs at the Soyal (Soyalawgwu) ceremony to compel the sun to reverse its southward retreat after the time of the winter solstice—an effort which is, of course, successful.

In figure 19 the central figure may represent one of several Hopi supernaturals, including Avachhoya (Avatshoya), Spotted-corn Kachina or Shula-witsi (Solaawitsi), a hunter. Both appear in various ceremonies and are characterized by painted circles or spots on their torsos.

In figure 20 a fully caparisoned warrior, similar to some shown in modern paintings and ceremonies, appears to the right of a sinuous "squash maiden," who dances behind him. That she is an unmarried woman is indicated by the whorls of hair at each side of her head. She may perhaps be associated with Patun (Patang), the Squash Kachina, although the latter is always male.

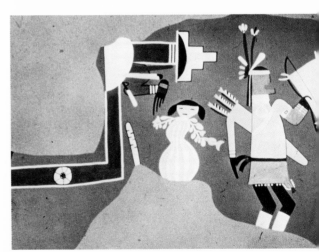

Fig. 21. Awatovi, Test 14, Room 2, Right Wall, Design No. 6.

Fig. 22. Awatovi, Room 788, Right Wall, Design No. 4.

In figure 21 the central figure, wearing a conical cap embellished with the imprint of a bear paw and carrying a shield, with bow and arrows, may represent one of the twin Hopi War Gods.

In figure 22 is almost certainly shown Ahöla kachina, who appears at the Powamu (*Powamuya*) ceremony and symbolizes the coming of the sun. Powamu (or "Bean Dance") occurs in February, and its purpose is the renovation of the earth for another planting season and the celebration of the return of the kachinas.

In figure 23 is a group of several personages. The one at the lower left is identifiable as Kokopelli (*Kookopölö*), a character who appears widely throughout the New World, and is distinguished by his humped back and his phallic ostentation. He is often depicted playing a flute and is then referred to as the Humpbacked Flute Player, but his more ribald role in Hopi ceremonials is that of a comic seducer of girls and a bringer of babies.

The upside-down figure above Kokopelli probably represents his female companion, Kokopell Mana (*Kokopöl Mana*), whose mask is decorated in the manner shown here.

The technology used in rendering the various styles of design seems not to have changed with time or among different craftsmen, although variations in skill can be noted. Paint was almost always applied as a solid cover over areas which were usually outlined with narrow borders of a contrasting color. The outlining was apparently applied after the body of the element had been completed. Rarely was a spatter technique used and almost never was there an attempt at shading or perspective.

It was not possible to determine whether a preliminary layout was scratched on the surface as a guide in constructing the design. The symmetry and balance with which most designs were arranged within the available field might seem to demand such advance planning, but in the light of the skill shown by modern Pueblo potters in painting their vessels wholly by eye and without preliminary guidelines, it seems probable that the ancient muralists may also have worked freehand.

The practice of painting kiva walls is old and widespread in the Pueblo Southwest. The earliest recorded samples, dated at around A.D. 900-1100, are very elemental series of geometric figures and hardly compare with the intricate pictorial murals of the sixteenth and seventeenth centuries found in Hopi and other Pueblo kivas in the Rio Grande area.

At Kuaua, now maintained as Coronado State Monument, twenty well-preserved mural paintings were recovered and copied at the University of New Mexico, and a definitive report has been written about them by Dr. Bertha P. Dutton (1962). The paintings from Kuaua were usually more freely drawn and more loosely arranged than were their Hopi counterparts, and they exhibited less static and carefully planned patterns. Dr. Dutton has connected them with prehistoric events at Zuñi and has interpreted them in terms of Zuñi legend and folklore.

By far the largest and most spectacular assemblage of kiva wall paintings, however, was found at a sixteenth-century pueblo called Pottery Mound in the valley of the Rio Puerco northwest of Albuquerque. At this village a mass of more than 800 individual design fragments from seventeen kivas were excavated under the direction of Dr. Frank C. Hibben (1975). The paintings at Pottery Mound resembled those in the Hopi villages much more closely than did those at Kuaua, and in some instances the identity was so close as almost to suggest execution by a single artist or at least by one belonging to the same school.

While it is not possible or appropriate here to attempt detailed analysis, it is enough to emphasize the widespread cultural and ceremonial dynamics that have pervaded the Pueblo world from early times until the present. The practice of kiva wall painting survives today at least among some Pueblos. One of the most comprehensive monographs on the subject is the *Hopi Journal* of Alexander M. Stephen, who lived among the Hopi for several years during the 1880s and 1890s. It is largely on the basis of Stephen's drawings and descriptions that interpretations by analogy have been made of the ancient paintings from Awatovi and Kawaika-a. In addition much insight has been derived from comparing direct observation of kachina costumes and activities during the public phases of modern Hopi dances with the ancient kiva mural portrayals of kachina figures. Furthermore, valuable testimony was gathered from the Hopi men who worked at the Awatovi excavation, other Hopi, such as Fred Kabotie and Elizabeth White, who have bridged the Indian and white worlds and want to help us understand the Hopi way, and many other "sidewalk superintendents" who came to watch.

Fig. 23. Awatovi, Room 529, Back Wall, Design 1 (detail).

# Conclusion

The discovery of ancient kiva mural paintings has provided a uniquely illuminating insight into the long continuity of Hopi religious symbolism and practice. These imaginative renderings emphasize the intimately dependent associations in the Hopi cosmos between mankind and Nature in all her forms—the animals, the plants, the winds, the rain—and the overpowering concern with fertility and life. Essential to human survival is the intercession of the kachinas, and the precarious balance between fulfillment and want is constantly reiterated through the realization of their annual retirement to their mountain home and their promised return in the coming spring.

But that their beneficent services may not be taken for granted is evident from the emphasis on mimetic actions and compulsive magic—to turn the sun around and to propitiate the forces of Nature. Without these things the delicate balance between Man and his world would collapse, and The People could no longer be.

Watson Smith
*Peabody Museum of Archaeology and Ethnology*
*Harvard University*

# Kachina: Window to the Hopi World

# by Dorothy K. Washburn

The Hopi people live in small villages on three sandstone mesa remnants which are part of the arid erosional escarpment called the Colorado Plateau in northern Arizona. From the time of first contact with the Spanish, the Hopi have been known by a number of appellations. Coronado and his group referred to these people as "Tusayan," a word apparently derived from "Tucano," which is the name Coronado gave to one of the Hopi villages. Since this time, many explorers, travelers, missionaries and anthropologists have used the term Tusayan to refer to the area occupied by the Hopi as well as to the people themselves. "Moqui" is a derogatory term for the Hopi which was first used by the Spanish and which unfortunately is still sometimes employed.

The proper name for these people is "Hopi," from their word *Hopi sinom*, which means "little people of peace." The Hopi are Uto-Aztecan speakers who, according to archaeological evidence, first began arriving at the mesas almost 900 years ago. In addition to the history revealed by archaeologists, the Hopi have a mythological explanation of their genesis which has been carefully passed orally through generations of Hopi. That the archaeological evidence gathered seems to discount the origin myth does not negate the vast metaphorical significance that this myth has for explaining reality to Hopi children as they grow up.

According to most accounts, the Hopi people, unhappy with their life in the Underworld, solicited the assistance of spirit powers who came as birds and animals to help them find the exit to a better world. Successful discovery by the shrike of a hole in the sky and growth of a giant reed planted by a chipmunk enabled the Hopi to enter this world. Spider Woman, the deity of the earth, and two Hurung Whuti (*Huru'ung Wuuti*), deities of the East and West who own turquoise, coral and seashell, created the Hopi men and women before the emergence and then led them in their wanderings to find a new home after the emergence.

Fig. 24. Tunei-nili (Small River) Kachina. Photographed by H. F. Robinson. Courtesy of the Museum of New Mexico, Santa Fe 21735.

# Symbolic Aspects of the Kachina in Hopi Culture

*We stay up and sing the sacred songs all night to purify ourselves so that our dancing and our prayers can do good for everyone.*

Alonzo Quavehema
"Rare Glimpse into the Evolving Way of the Hopi" by James K. Page, Jr.
*Smithsonian* November 1975

Fig. 25. Kiva Hatchway, Walpi, First Mesa. Photographed by Joseph Mora, 1904-1906. Courtesy of John R. Wilson.

The events of Hopi life—both sacred and secular—are laden with symbolic meaning. Places, colors and images all carry metaphorical implications and thus serve to enrich what are to the Western eye apparently severe environmental and marginal living conditions. Indeed, it is the very variety in ways of manifesting a symbolic event that promotes excitement and anticipation. Identical ceremonies are portrayed differently in each village. Costumes vary constantly and this is clearly attested by wide variations in the representation of any particular kachina tihu (*katsin tihu*). Thus dancers and events are displays of a constant stream of different, creative interpretations of the basic principles in Hopi life and thought.

For example, in symbolic terms the origin myth is, in effect, reenacted in every ceremonial. The tradition of the Hopi emergence through a reed into this world is kept alive by the presence of a sipapu (*sipaapu*). Literally, this is a small hole in the kiva floor next to the central firepit or a niche in the wall. Figuratively, it is the place of emergence upon birth and reentry upon death for the Hopi people. The position of the kiva as an underground chamber with egress via a hole in the roof can also be seen as metaphorical of Hopi prior existence in an Underworld and their emergence into this world through a hole in the sky.

Because kivas house some of the most sacred and important preparations for ceremonials, the participants in these activities transform themselves mentally from Hopi fathers and farmers to kachinas (*katsinam*) and priests who have accepted the serious duty of transferring Hopi prayers to the deities. In effect, every person who exits from the kiva is symbolically beginning a new life.

During the period of preparation which always precedes every public dance, the Hopi pray and perform cleansing rites each day before altars erected in the kivas. Pahos (*paavaho*), or prayer sticks, are made, blessed and then deposited at shrines around the village. On the last day when the men exit from the kiva as kachinas, they are, in effect, exiting reborn in a new guise. Each ceremonial is thus both a recreation of the Hopi as one people and a transformation of each Hopi as a kachina. The continual schedule of dances between the winter solstice in December and the summer solstice in June serves to remind and instill this sense of past and future direction in the Hopi people.

The importance of the purification process should be emphasized. Dancers wash their hair before ceremonials. The actual marriage ceremony consists of washing the hair of the bride and groom. All participants in a mud fight between the families of the bride and groom wash themselves and the whole interior of the house after the "battle." A new baby is washed every fifth day and on the twentieth day after birth when it is named and presented to the sun.

These cleansings all take place at critical transitions when a Hopi is passing from the secular to the sacred world in a ceremonial, or when a Hopi is moving into a new life stage, such as birth or marriage. At each point it is necessary to cleanse one-

Fig. 26. Hemis Kachina with spruce ruff carrying cattails. Courtesy of the Smithsonian Institution, National Anthropological Archives 79-4289.

self of all past feelings and associations in order to begin life anew.

Furthermore, many of these purification and other preparatory rituals occur before dawn. Dawn is a very important point in every Hopi's day, since the coming of the sun presages a new day, and a new day with sun brings warmth and thus growth potential to the earth. Thus, it is important to be cleansed in thought and body in order to receive the benevolent action of the deities and the beneficial powers of the sun and rain.

The metaphorical aspects of the sipapu and kiva are but a small fraction of the rich symbolism which has grown with Hopi tradition. The kachinas—messengers and intermediaries between men and gods—literally wear their world. The environment of the Hopi people is, to many passersby, a bleak, dry uninviting land. The Hopi, however, have successfully wrested a living from the sand dunes and washes for centuries. Although they are considered to be a sedentary farming culture, the Hopi range widely in all directions to utilize the rich array of resources and they thankfully symbolize these in their ceremonial costuming.

The San Francisco peaks to the west of the mesas are not only the home of the kachinas during the winter months, but also the

Fig. 27. Tortoise shell rattle, No. 165.

Fig. 28. Polik Manas at Walpi, First Mesa. Photographed by Joseph Mora, 1904-1906. Courtesy of John R. Wilson.

source of spruce boughs which kachinas and manas wear as collars, hand and ankle ornaments. It is significant that, although juniper and pinyon are available in the mesa area, the Hopi journey to the mountains to obtain spruce. Thus spruce is worn as a symbolic recognition of that part of the Hopi world.

Likewise, the tortoiseshell rattles that kachinas wear on the backs of their legs below the knee reflect Hopi thanks to the ponds and spring areas where tortoises live and which supply that basic necessity of life—water. Eagle and turkey feathers, prized accoutrements worn symbolically on the head (i.e., on kachina masks), or held in the hand (i.e., attached to rattles or prayer sticks), mimic the wish to carry airborne prayers from the Hopi. Terraced wooden tablitas, the mask superstructure seen most characteristically on the Polik Mana (*Palhikw Mana*) and Hemis Kachinas (*Hemis katsina*) or on the Butterfly dancer, carry geometric representations of clouds, lightning, rain, seeds and corn as if their graphic portrayal will serve to reinforce and ensure the transmittal of prayers for these things to the deities.

One other way the kachinas "wear their world" is through use of the six different colors which relate to the six different sacred directions. North is represented by blue or green, west by yellow, south by red, east by white, zenith by multicolors and nadir by black. The Hopi acknowledge the resources and weather which come from each of these directions in the colors of the costumes and other religious paraphernalia. For example, on kiva altars, the corn ears, arranged to point in each direction, have kernels of the appropriate color. A dancer's neck ruff is green; the sashes are red, green and black, or white. Both the kilts and shawls often have multicolored embroidered designs

on the edges which utilize all major directional colors. Typical designs of terraced clouds with rain, butterflies or kachina faces are black, green, yellow, and red on a white background.

But who are these masked dancers, called kachinas, who first appear in the village at the Soyal (*Soyalanguu*) celebration at the winter solstice in December to bless the kivas for another year and then leave seven months later to "sleep" in the San Francisco peaks? Hopi oral history tells us that in the Underworld the Hopi people lived side by side with the kachinas. It became apparent, however, that the Hopi were taking the solicitous actions and prayers of the kachinas for granted. The kachinas decided to leave the Hopi, but before their departure, they taught the Hopi all the necessary sacred ritual and paraphernalia so that Hopi men could "impersonate" the kachinas during the growing and harvest season and thus continue to obtain kindly attentions from the deities.

The kachinas are present for about seven months: from Soyal, when they reappear to open a new growing season; through the late February Powamu (*Powamuy*) celebration, when the kachinas grow bean sprouts in their kivas as symbolic encouragement for the germination of crops to be planted later in the spring; through the many mixed and line dances during the spring months, when the kachinas dance to implore wind, lightning, rain and sunshine for the crops; until the climatic *Niman* celebration, when the Hopi have an early sweet-corn harvest to thank the kachinas for all their help. After this finale the kachinas return to their winter home in the San Francisco peaks.

The asymmetric relationship between the celebration of an event and the actual occurrence of an event is uniquely Hopi. For example, although the actual planting and germination of crops do not occur until May and June, the Hopi begin to perform rituals for this event at Powamu. One of the key symbolic preparations is the enactment of the germination process by force-growing beans in heated kivas (*Natwanta*). All of nature is still asleep on the windblown and snow-covered mesas, and it is so cold that most ceremonials have to be held indoors. Only the Hopi, in concert with the kachinas, are concerned with the coming growing season.

The constant series of kiva and plaza dances and races after Powamu in the early spring months are all held prior to the principal planting months of May and June. Again these advance preparations are considered necessary to ensure that the wind, thunder, lightning, rain and sun come at the right time. Early winds bring clouds and thus rain, but winds too late will whip the delicate shoots to shreds and cover them with sand. Rain in July and August is vital for the final maturation of the corn, but rain too hard or too soon will wash away the tiny plants.

Likewise, an asymmetric relationship is present at Niman, the second major ceremonial of the Hopi year, which is a celebration of the harvest. Niman occurs in late July, but this is two months before the main corn is harvested in September. Small plots of corn, which will be harvested specifically for Niman, are planted early in the spring in areas protected from late frosts. The large

*I had planted a patch of early sweet corn in April. We had to dig holes four inches deep and cover the grains two inches, leaving a shallow pit above the seeds which served as a pocket to catch the suns rays...I fitted little grass and twig windbreaks around each plant, or collected old tin cans, opened both ends, and set them over the seedlings. The cans were better, for they also protected the plants from mice and worms. I wanted this corn ripe for the Niman dance in July.*

Don Talayesva
*Sun Chief*

*It is dancing day. All the people are very happy. They have brought some corn and watermelons for the children... In the afternoon, just when the kachina stop dancing, for their dinner, there is a big rain storm. As soon as they eat their dinner, they start dancing again. It is still raining. Everybody gets wet, the kachina also. The water is running. We can see the water everywhere, the water is running all over the fields. So we are very glad...*

Crow-Wing
*A Pueblo Indian Journal*
July 27, 1921

Fig. 29. Peaches drying on Walpi rooftops. Photographed by Joseph Mora, 1904-1906. Courtesy of
John Wilson.

quantities of corn and other food given away at this dance symbolically represent the Hopi's hope for the size of the actual harvest yet to come. Indeed, Niman highlights the Hopi concern with
fertility by celebrating its fruits. Furthermore, the production of
bounteous amounts of food means the continuation of the Hopi
people.

Complementary with but characteristically in opposition to
the idea of asymmetry in timing preparations for an event and the
actual occurrence of an event, is the sense of circularity inherent
in Hopi thought and action. The symbolic exit of all Hopi from
the sipapu and subsequent reentry upon death simulate a circular path. The Hopi believe that when a person dies his spirit is carried up to the clouds and falls again as rain. Thus the rain, which
falls to the earth and nurtures life which then grows and dies, creates this same idea of recirculation.

During the seven-month period of constant ritual activity
between Powamu and Niman, the kachinas are the principal
caretakers of the Hopi people. They appear early enough in the
season to begin sending the Hopi's prayers to the deities and,
equally important, to "police" the Hopi themselves so that their
behavior and minds are pure and honest.

Very early in the lives of the Hopi children the kachinas make
a strong impression. At Powamu the Soyoko (*So'yoko*) visit all
homes with young uninitiated children and demand that the little
girls grind corn and the boys catch mice. They return after a few
days demanding these foodstuffs and, if insufficient, threaten to
kidnap the children. This display is but one of a number of ways
that children are brought to respect and obey the kachinas.

Kachinas mete out discipline to adults as well as children.
After Powamu the springs around the mesas have to be drained
and cleaned of the silts which have accumulated during the past
year. Although the work parties are composed of volunteers, this
is really one of the many obligatory tasks every Hopi male must
perform. Kachinas are present at these events to ensure that all

*When you've been watching the kachi-
nas all day, absorbing the rhythm of
the stamping feet and turtleshell rattles,
inspired by the music of voices in unison,
muffled beneath the masks, you can't
help feeling the sincerity and dedication
behind it all.*

Fred Kabotie
*Fred Kabotie: Hopi Indian Artist*

who use the springs are present; laggards are "whipped" into action by kachinas with yucca fronds.

Most visible for the visiting non-Hopi are the spring and early summer dance activities of the kachinas. Normally these are one-day public dances preceded by a week of preparations. These dances, which consist of four or more appearances of a line of kachina dancers throughout the day separated by pauses for rest, lunch and clown activity, represent the culmination of four days of intensive purification ritual by all men involved. Unless the participants' minds are pure, the prayers and dance will not be effective. Throughout the spring, members of different kivas prepare and present these dances for good weather and good crops. Each time they appear, wearing all the symbols of fertility, growth

Fig. 30. Mixed Dance at Hano, First Mesa, showing Kowako (Rooster Kachina), Avachhoya (Spotted Corn Kachina) and Mashanta (Flower Kachina). Photographed by Joseph Mora, 1904-1906. Courtesy of John R. Wilson.

Fig. 31. Soyoko at Walpi, First Mesa. From left to right: Hahai-i Wu-uti, Tahaum Soyoko, Soyok Mana, Soyok Wu-uti, Wiharu, three Nata-askas, Wiharu, three Heheyas. Photographed by James Mooney, February, 1893. Courtesy of the Smithsonian Institution, National Anthropological Archives 1824D.

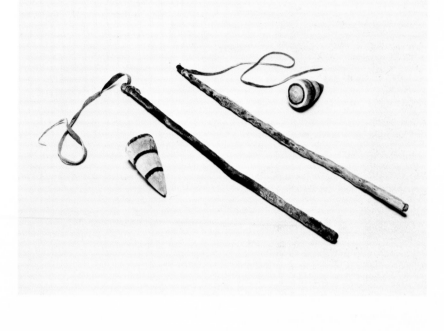

Fig. 32. Shinney stick, No. 123, and balls, No. 124-125.

Fig. 33. Tops with whips, No. 126-127.

*The old man said the game had to be played four days, because they had to tear the ball and let the seed come out, so it will be well and they will have good crops in the summer... This game is not played for money or anything, but for the crops.*

Crow-Wing
*A Pueblo Indian Journal*
February 1, 1921

and harvest, it is as if they are recreating life and thus encouraging and ensuring its continuity.

This focus on fertility is also expressed symbolically in many other ways than through the activity of the kachinas. For example, the game of shinny (*nahoytatatsya*) that two teams of boys play during the spring months carries more than casual entertainment value. It is significant not only that it is played only during the spring months when the crops are being planted but also that the buckskin balls are filled with seeds. It is said that if the boys do not break the ball within four days, the crops will not germinate. In effect, the breaking of the ball symbolizes the germination of the crops, while failure to break the ball presages a difficult growing season ahead.

Reinforcing this emphasis on germination rather than sport is the absence of prizes for the team who finally breaks the buckskin ball. The absence of awards for winners in many Hopi games is a reminder that most games are basically not competitive in nature and are not designed to aggrandize either an individual or a team. Rather, they are played for a greater purpose—the well-being of the entire Hopi community. Winning and losing is irrelevant; skill and prowess are important only insofar as they relate to furthering the theme of growth in Hopi life.

Among other games which symbolically encourage growth are spinning tops during March, the month of winds. The humming noise produced by the spinning simulates the sound of wind and this expresses the Hopi's hope for winds which will bring clouds laden with rain.

Races pitting Hopi men against kachinas are said to encourage the sun to rise higher in the sky. The faster a man runs, the sooner the sun will bring those long hot summer days so essential for corn growth and maturation. Unlike our concept of sports-

Fig. 34. Wawarus (racers), Sichomovi, First Mesa. Photographed by Joseph Mora 1904-1906. Courtesy of John R. Wilson.

manship where winning is all important, the Hopi are not concerned with being first, but with being fastest. Each Hopi runner is competing with Nature, not with other runners, since his focus is on impressing the sun with his need for good weather.

Some races are held with only Hopi men racing against each other; others involve kachinas challenging men to short races. In the latter case, if a Hopi man loses, the kachinas may strike him with a yucca whip, cover his face with ashes, cut his hair, or perform some other prank. This activity not only elevates the kachinas to an enforcer role, but also demonstrates the importance of speed, ostensibly to outrun the kachina, but really to show heartfelt desire for the blessings the kachinas can bestow.

From this perspective we can understand how and why the kachinas are so important to the Hopi people and why, although many superficial aspects of American culture have been adopted such as automobiles for faster transport and jeans and tee shirts for everyday wear, each year the Hopi leave this whirlwind world of change and reenact the sacred rituals of fertility and harvest. As long as they live on the Arizona mesas, the Hopi need to propitiate the deities for good weather and bountiful crops to survive. The San Francisco Mountains, everpresent as distant peaks in the western sky, are a metaphorical "rock of Gibraltar" for the Hopi. They are always there providing a home for the kachinas, who, given sincere thoughts and prayers of the Hopi, will always return to help the "people of peace" reproduce themselves and their crops for another year.

*...all life is a planting, a growing, and a harvesting...prayers are tangible things when properly conceived, and capable of coming to abundant fruition and seedtime.*

Polingaysi Qoyawayma
*No Turning Back*

# Secular Aspects of Hopi Life

Family relationships and social responsibilities comprise the other, but complementary side of Hopi life. The clan substructure, which provides an extensive series of relatives through the female line, organizes every Hopi's activities into a continual series of reciprocal gift and work obligations. Each Hopi child is born into an extended family, which means that many more people than the mother and father are responsible for and responsive to the care and training of the child. Ceremonial fathers guide children through initiation into the kachina cult and secret societies. Paternal aunts assist in the first naming ceremony and later wedding preparations. Maternal uncles are the children's principal disciplinarians.

In all these crucial transition points in a Hopi's life whereby he or she is given more ritual knowledge or reaches an age where he or she assumes additional work responsibilities, persons outside the basic mother-father-sibling family are responsible. In turn, this creates lifelong bonds of friendship as well as obligation which can be used when one person needs help weaving a wedding dress, making quantities of piki for a dance, or supplementing family food stores in case of harvest failure. Although dollars buy gasoline, tinned goods and tennis shoes, the important aspects of Hopi life are still acquired by reciprocal exchanges of work and resources. This self-perpetuating succession of obligations which characterizes Hopi daily life in both the secular and sacred spheres is one of the strongest factors behind the continuity of Hopi culture.

Many of these procedures involved in family living, particularly those related to the transitions in a person's life, are performed with as much symbolic solemnity as are those which occur during kachina or nonkachina dances. For example, the lengthy wedding preparations involve a series of food and gift exchanges between the bride's and groom's families. All items and events in this process carry symbolic significance relating to fertility, growth and life. The cornmeal which the bride and her relatives grind for the groom is hand ground, never store-bought, and contains special additions to ensure long life. Likewise, the tassels on the white braided wedding sash which the groom's relatives make for the bride contain special things which make it perfect and thus ensure that the marriage will be a happy and long-lasting relationship.

Even certain actions in events carry rich symbolic meaning. For example, the throwing of mud in the mock fight between the women of the bride's and groom's families not only strengthens ties of maternal and paternal aunts but also highlights the importance of water. The making of mud requires quantities of water, and since water is essential to life, a mud fight—where large amounts of water are used—displays, in effect, the symbolic hope that there will always be water and therefore life. Since the reproductive powers of women are central to the continuity of life, it is fitting that the mud fight is held during a transition ceremony where a woman is being prepared to enter a new life role, the focal point of which is raising a family.

*Corn Grinding Song:*

*Oh, for a heart as pure as pollen on*
*   corn blossoms,*
*And for a life as sweet as honey*
*   gathered from the flowers,*
*And beautiful as butterflies in sunshine.*
*May I do good, as Corn has done good*
*   for my people*
*Through all the days that were.*
*Until my task is done and evening falls,*
*Oh, Mighty Spirit, hear my grinding*
*   song.*

Polingaysi Qoyawayma
*No Turning Back*

For men, preparing for and dancing in a ceremonial becomes both a symbolic gesture of cleansing and separation from this world to enter the world of a kachina and an actual cathartic release from daily quarrels with neighbors and kin. Because everyone in the kiva is making prayer sticks and refurbishing dance paraphernalia and, in this process is sharing ideas, materials and assistance, individual enmities are submerged in collective effort toward a common goal—ensuring the well-being and thus the continuity of a Hopi community.

The above paragraphs have but briefly touched on some aspects of Hopi life which are critical to the characterization of the Hopi as a unique culture. In the Hopi way, kachinas are essential beings which supplicate life and thus survival for the culture. Despite the many incursions of western civilization, the Hopi continue to rely ultimately not on modern technology, but on the power of the kachina.

Dorothy K. Washburn
*Chairman, Department of Anthropology*
*California Academy of Sciences*

# HOPI SOCIAL ORGANIZATION

## by John Connelly

The Hopi people live in the high semiarid Colorado Plateau country of northeastern Arizona. As noted by the late Harold S. Colton in 1934, the Hopi people do not constitute a tribe in the usual sense of the term. The prominent characteristics encompassing the whole of the Hopi population, approximately five thousand people, are a shared pueblo-type life-style and socio-religious ceremonialism but a language which is entirely distinct from that of other pueblo peoples. (The Tewa-speaking people of the small Hopi community of Hano represent a language exception, although Hano people share the common pueblo life-style.)

Just as the concept of tribe is inapplicable to Hopi society so too are the terms pueblo, town or village. The connotations of these terms have led to expectations of a Euro-American political order in the residency groups which not only does not exist but also is antithetical to the Hopi sense of social order. The generalization prevalent in the history of American social development that "big is good"—ergo "bigger is better"—runs counter to the Hopi view that "balance is best." The precarious natural environment and limited resources in water and arable land did not support large populations but, rather, small community associations which were easily deployable. The breakup of the Great Pueblos in archaeological times may illustrate this principle of survival.

The American response to the magnitude, the harsh beauty, the cruel threat of the natural environment of the Colorado Plateau country was to seek mastery and control. The Hopi, on the other hand, sought harmony with this environment. The stereotypical view of the Hopi as a benign, harmonious, peaceful people is, on the whole, a romantic illusion but not without some substance. Happiness lies not in a remote hereafter in this or another universe of being but in a persistent now. The quality of the persistent present includes the Hopi future, and that quality demands constant, immediate caring. In Hopi social and ceremonial organization there is to be found a mode of associational behavior which exemplifies Hopi perceptions of harmony, of balance and of the immediacy of task. It should be noted that just as there is no "waiting for heaven" in Hopi thought, there is also no lost "Garden of Eden" in the social mythology of Hopi past. The lore of the past is dominated by emphasis upon the evil of neglect of responsibility and upon migrations of people seeking a better place for a good life.

Fig. 35. First Mesa, with Walpi in the foreground. Photographed by Peter Dechert, 1977. Courtesy of Peter Dechert 77A 30/6.

# Communities and Community Clusters

Fig. 36. Shongopavi, Second Mesa. Photographed by Peter Dechert, 1977. Courtesy of Peter Dechert 77A 34/2.

Fig. 37. Shipaulovi, Second Mesa. Photographed by Peter Dechert, 1977. Courtesy of Peter Dechert 77A 31/11.

Fig. 38. Mishongnovi, Second Mesa. Photographed by Peter Dechert, 1977. Courtesy of Peter Dechert 77A 32/12.

The idea of place carries with it identity and responsibility and belonging. The most visible units of Hopi social organization, which, in the literature on Hopi, have been termed pueblos, towns or villages, are *places*: (-vi, -bi or -pi endings are translated "place") Walpi (*Walpi*), "place of the gap"; Sichomovi (*Sitsom'ovi*), "hill place where flowers grow"; Hano (*Haano* or *Hanoki*, Tewa word for *anopi*), "place of the eastern people"; Shongopavi (*Songoopavi*), "water place where reeds grow"; Shipaulovi (*Supawlavi*), "place of mosquitoes"; Mishongnovi (*Musangnuvi*), "place of the dark man"; Oraibi (*Orayvi*), "place of orai" (a type of rock); Kyakotsmovi (*Kiqötsmovi*), "place of the hill of ruins"; Hotevilla (*Ho'atvela*), "a slope of junipers" or perhaps "a scraped back"; Bakavi or Bakabi (*Paaqavi*), "place of (a type of) reeds"; Moenkopi (*Munqapi*), "place where water flows."

These places, these residency sites or settlements, located on the southern fingers of a huge eroded upland, Black Mesa, have become identified in American times as the villages of East or First Mesa, the villages of Middle or Second Mesa and the villages of West or Third Mesa. Until recently they were viewed by outsiders as autonomous or semiautonomous towns or villages. There was a Euro-American assumption of a "chief," or authoritarian figure of government or political control. Hopi perception of government was in distribution of responsibility rather than concentration of authority. The fact that the settlement sites were named encouraged the outsiders' ideas of their separate identities and obscured the pattern of their reciprocal relationships. In both historic and prehistoric times—the former in recorded events and the latter in oral tradition—the people came to occupy their places of residency and they acquired their lands for farming in return for commitments of responsibility.

The First Mesa villages—Walpi, Sichomovi and Hano—form a cluster of residency settlements. Walpi is the prime or mother village; Sichomovi is the satellite, or colony; and Hano is the guard village for both Walpi and Sichomovi. The Tewa people of Hano came to Hopi country following the Pueblo Revolt of 1680. They petitioned for a place to live and lands to farm, in exchange for which they committed themselves to serve as guards for the Hopi, a function still referred to by both groups. For the residents of Sichomovi, the adult initiation into the ceremonial societies takes place at Walpi, thus identifying Sichomovi as a colony. These linking relationships establish patterns of interdependency between the three communities.

The Second Mesa villages, with Shongopavi the mother, Shipaulovi the colony the Mishongnovi the guard, form another cluster of interdependent communities.

The Third Mesa villages appear at first glance to be of a somewhat different character. Oraibi was throughout both the Spanish and the American periods conspicuous for its size and also its location. Whereas other villages were moved to the mesa tops for security after the Pueblo Revolt, Oraibi was already on top of the mesa, and according to archaeological evidence had been there since at least A.D. 1150.

The segmentation process, characteristic of Hopi organization, appeared to be arrested at Oraibi during historic times. Did its mesa top provide a sense of security from raiding bands of Utes or Navajos, and later from the possible return of the Spanish? We can only speculate. We do know, however, that Oraibi became a socially explosive community with a population far larger than could be accommodated by its domestic water supply or accessible farm lands. Failure to segment built up internal tension and factionalism and led to competition (in Hopi eyes, an evil) for power and control. Although a small farming colony had developed at Moenkopi in the late 1870s and there had begun a drift of population to the site which was to become the present Kyakotsmovi, these were insufficient to release the population pressure and provide for a manageable dispersal. Undoubtedly, American missionaries, traders and government personnel also affected the situation, but the explosive ingredients were internal. The shattering division of the community in the fall of 1906 led to the founding of Hotevilla, Bakavi and Kyakotsmovi and eventually the division of the colony of Moenkopi into two communities.

Of importance to the study of Hopi social organization of Third Mesa is the increasingly pronounced trend of clustering of communities over the past seventy years. Kyakotsmovi (New Oraibi), Upper Moenkopi and Bakavi tend toward alignment—an alignment of convenience, however, rather than dependency. Their warranty for being (and therefore dependency) is primarily upon external agencies and resources such as the federal government and various religious missionary groups.

Among the other three settlements, even though scars of conflict remain, the cluster affinity of Oraibi, Lower Moenkopi and Hotevilla reflects characteristics of the native Hopi pattern. Warranty for their existence is dependent upon recognition of Oraibi as the mother village, with Lower Moenkopi its colony and Hotevilla having increasingly become identified as the guardian of Hopi orthodoxy for the mother village.

The clustering patterns of Hopi communities demonstrate the balancing characteristics of Hopi social order between the needs for segregation and the needs for integration. These residency settlement clusters are unnamed but are clearly discernible and functional. They are the largest units of social structure within Hopi society.

Fig. 39. Old Oraibi, Third Mesa. Photographed by Peter Dechert. Courtesy of the Southwest Foundation for Audio-Visual Resources SAR 10/16.

Fig. 40. Hotevilla, Third Mesa with terraced gardens below spring. Photographed by Peter Dechert. Courtesy of Peter Dechert 77A 36/1.

# Clans and Phratries

Along with the common pueblo culture and language, there is an interlinking matrilineal clan system which provides intercommunity linkages throughout Hopi society.

A Hopi individual is born into the clan of his or her mother, and acquires a corps of allied kin through the father. The clans, like the settlements, are named and are clustered in unnamed groups—exogamous phratries. The clan-phratry system provides a place for the individual in relation to other people. The individual is a kinsman to all individuals belonging to his or her clan, whether they are in his or her own community of residence or elsewhere.

In the origin and migration myths and the lore of clans there are accounts of the clans' backgrounds, commitments and conditions of admission into Hopi society. In the lore and myths of the Hopi, the Bear Clan people were the first arrivals in Hopi country and took possession of the land for all the people. Subsequent arrivals were assigned occupancy places in the community and farming areas in exchange for the performance of specific ceremonies or services to the community. The lore describes all clans as coming to a single village, a theoretical original settlement, and this perception still persists at Shongopavi on Second Mesa, where the Bear Clan remains vigorous. Rationale is developed, however, to explain the dispersal of clans. One example is the story of a quarrel between two Bear Clan brothers and the departure of one to the place which came to be called Oraibi; another is the account of the founding of Shipaulovi by clan segments from Shongopavi, who were assigned to conceal and protect Hopi ceremonies against the return of the Spanish. Whatever the explanations, clans have dispersed. The great numbers of small archaeological sites throughout the country, and clan identification with particular ones, confirm the lore's emphasis upon migrations of small bands of people. These migration stories may reflect a buried social consciousness of origins in a seed-gathering, pre-agricultural past or of less ancient moves caused by drought or other natural disasters. The dispersal of clans, however, gives support to the theory of segmentation as an essential in Hopi social organization.

To offset the hurts, the angers, the fears entailed in segmentation, associations of affinity and interdependence developed a balancing reintegration. Kinship ties provided mechanisms for appeasing the angers and giving kinsmen a sense of worth and affinity, even though separated by the necessity for relieving the population pressure on community land and water resources. Migrations of lineages, some tenuous, some permanent, have taken place in living memory.

Looking at the numbers of clans and phratries in the prime villages of the three cluster areas gives us some sense of clan dispersal. The Bear and Spider Clans of Walpi having become extinct, there remain fourteen extant clans in eleven phratry groups. At Shongopavi, where the Kachina (katsina) Clan and the clans of its phratry group have become extinct, ten clans, in three phratry groups, remain. At Oraibi, where the Bear Clan has just recently become extinct, there were recorded at the time of its break-up thirty clans in eleven phratry groups.

Although over fifty clans (in about a dozen phratry groups) have been identified, some have been noted as extinct or recently extinct, some as migrant, and others are of such vague reference as to be questionable. Although the clan system permeates the whole of Hopi society, it is not actually an incorporating element. There may be no specifics concerning migrations within the memory of any living individuals of a given clan, but there is a pervasive sense of outward going rather than incoming. There is a pacification process under which reciprocal courtesy and hospitality—appeasing and pleasing behaviors—blur painful memories of separation, best left undisturbed. In effect, the clan system provides links with kinsmen which are reciprocal with a minimal level of obligation.

Internal to the Hopi communities, clan ties become highly obligatory, as will be seen when we examine households and lineages.

The generalized kinship behavior of clansmen outside the community of residence becomes intensified within the community. Here the individual is given life, position, protection and ultimately responsibility. Understanding the dynamics of clan relationships relies upon knowledge of the subunits of the clan, the household and the lineage.

The clans are matrilineal and matrilocal. Traditionally the head of the household was its senior woman and she was attended and supported by her daughters, whose husbands provided economic support, and by her grandchildren. Upon call she had her brothers, who, while living in their marital households, were readily available. Although a child born into a household knows his biological mother, he also knows her sisters as mothers, the same kinship term being used for both. He also knows the offspring of all of these women as his brothers and sisters. There are also uncles (mother's brothers) in-residence or, if married, frequent visitors. All of these individuals, including his maternal grandmother and her sisters, are of the same clan. His father, although of a different clan, provides an additional array of supportive kin. It is the immediate in-resident maternal kin, however, who provide the sense of his belonging, of being a prized member of an in-group.

Because of the harsh character of the environment—too early or too late frost, summer floods, drought, wind- and sandstorms—the threat to survival has been ever present in Hopi history. Hopi response has been to explore and cultivate all potentials of this natural environment and of human capacity to cope with it. It is in the household where the spirit of cooperative work on the tasks of survival is nurtured and the capacity of each human potential is cultivated.

# Households and Lineages

The people are getting ready for the dance. Some men and boys are going for wood, some are killing steers and sheep. Wagons are being driven down for water. So everybody is very busy. Some women are baking piki and some baking bread. And women go to the house of the man who is head of the dance to bake piki and bread, for the dance. And so everybody is helping. Because any time anyone may need help, therefore all help one another.

Crow-Wing
A Pueblo Indian Journal
April 7, 1921

Generally the members of the prime lineage and prime household occupy the clanhouse. It is here that the ceremonial symbols and equipment are housed, where children learn of clan lore, tradition, commitment and responsibility, where infants are named and burial rites performed, where life begins and life ends.

A prime lineage of a clan may consist of more than a single descent line. If, in fact, it is reduced to a single line, it is in a precarious position. Within the prime lineage there is a prime descent line maintaining the clan-mother house or household. This descent line forms the core of the lineage and ideally is most secure when sustained by supportive secondary lines of descent. The secondary descent lines provide support services and, most important, insurance against clan extinction. (A clan becomes extinct with a generation of all-male births.)

The ideal prime lineage consists of a senior clan woman (*so'o*) who is the "clan-mother," with one or more brothers to handle the ritual and disciplinary roles of the group, and several married daughters with their husbands and children. Ideally, sons should be married into significant households of clans in other phratry groups, to establish protective alliances for the household and lineage. The senior male of the lineage is most often its disciplinarian and ritual head, with other males of his generation serving as aides. As males of the next generation come into full adulthood the disciplinarian role of the senior male is taken over and he comes to serve more in his counseling role, with increasing attention to ritual affairs and transmission of clan lore to his successor.

Additional descent lines, or lineages, peripheral to the prime line and its close aide line, can be carried as long as the resources of the whole group allow. But indications of rebellion against the prime household of the clan or excess demand upon the resources of the group as a whole require that peripheral lines be sloughed off. This is obviously a distressing experience for individuals of the excess lineage. It implies a devaluation and even abandonment. It must be pressed, however, to the point where dependency is alleviated by migration of at least part of a generation, unless new resources can be developed. A greater evil is the threat of competing claims upon the same resources, such as led to the explosive division of Oraibi. Far preferable, within Hopi life-style with its emphasis upon process, is gradual sloughing-off.

This segmentation process, though necessary, leaves hostile groups on the periphery of settlement, which cannot safely be left unameliorated. Most important to the separated group is the retention of Hopi identity, which is contained in clan membership. The mother household continues to acknowledge the kinship tie, providing a measure of pacification which can be furthered by other recognitions of the group's validity, such as assignment of ceremonial roles.

Sloughed-off descent lines may be nascent clan groups, as suggested by Mischa Titiev in his study of Oraibi (1944). This hypothesis suggests that member clans of a phratry may well have been originally sloughed-off lineages of clans. This theory is reinforced by the extension of kinship terminology to clans within a phratry and the rule of exogamy, which bans marriage between members of these clans. By such a technique the new clan would be required to develop its own resources and diminish demands upon existing resources. The acknowledged kinship tie serves to give members of the new group social location, in return for which they perform certain services for the mother group.

What is to be seen in the dynamics of the lines of descent is the continuous adjustment of people protecting their common security in order to maintain their clan group and their identity. Those individuals living and maintaining the clan house do so not for themselves alone but for all members of the clan in the community and theoretically for all members of the clan elsewhere. Their security is no greater than the security of all. As they receive support from other clan members, they concurrently are increasing their responsibilities for others. They are, in a real sense, the conservators of the clan identity and integrity. Deep in the lore of the past and maintained down to the present is the agreement which gave a place to live and land to farm to the clan and for which the clan committed itself to serve in a particular manner whether for the performance and preservation of a ceremony or for the protection of the community from assault.

Within the communities the clans occupy differing status positions. Looking beyond the charges and countercharges arising from the aberrant situation at the breakup of Oraibi, where competitive forces arose to disturb the social order, the social status arrangement of clans displays moderating, integrating characteristics by placing check on divisive competitive dispositions.

By tradition the Bear Clan holds the highest social status, based upon the belief that the Bear Clan arrived first in the area and negotiated agreements with all succeeding arrivals for places to reside and lands to farm—negotiations entailing commitment on the part of those who came later. Enforcement of the authority of the Bear Clan or its representative lay in maintaining a vigilant account of agreements and repeating generation after generation its understanding of commitments made. The subordinate clans were thus in defensive positions, having always to demonstrate the effectiveness of their commitments or explain away their failures in the face of the threat caused by drought, sandstorms, floods, marauding bands of outsiders or other causes in the large, harsh environment of Hopi country. Disputatiousness and scapegoating which rose in times of adversity did not leave the Bear Clan vulnerable to the same extent as the other clans.

To ameliorate intergroup tensions, interclan alliances are necessary. Marriage is an institution which provides for interclan alliances outside the network of natal kin in which an individual is located. Clansmen and members of exogamous associate clans are already within the kin group. Marriage brings disassociated groups into this affinity of kin. A woman eligible for marriage, despite any agreement she might have with a prospective husband, must be accepted by his mother and/or sisters. If the

*In the morning the Oraibi crier, Kelnimptiwa (Sand), called out that Kane's house was ready for plastering and asked all the women who wished to help to report there. Although it was a scorching hot day, nearly all of the pueblo's women showed up. Practically all of them could trace some relationship to Kane or his wife.*

Mischa Titiev
*The Hopi Indians of Old Oraibi*
September 1, 1933

*During the morning the crier called out requesting volunteers to begin grinding corn for Louise's wedding. Martha was one of the first to go because Luke, her husband, is Louise's half brother and a member of her (Greasewood) clan.*

Mischa Titiev
*The Hopi Indians of Old Oraibi*
November 1, 1933

cornmeal offering, which the bride carries to their house, is accepted, the bride-to-be remains in the house of the husband-to-be and demonstrates her capabilities as a homemaker to his maternal kin.

Acceptance here, however, is only partial acceptance, as his paternal kin arrive and challenge the decision with shouting criticism, taunts, derision not only of her but also of her newly won allies. There then ensues a ritualistic mud fight between his maternal and paternal kinswomen. The house of the groom's mother is left in great disarray and, theoretically, the prospective bride, to win the approval of the opposition, must demonstrate her capabilities by restoring the house to order. Actually she is given help by those who did battle for her and with her. The task completed, the groom's paternal kinswomen return, bringing gifts of cornmeal, piki and other foods and their approval of the marriage.

The rite performed to consolidate the marriage is quite simple: the mother of the bride and the mother of the groom wash the hair of the couple together in suds of soapweed (yucca), confirming the union. This ceremony initiates a series of reciprocal activities in which the clan kin of the bride and the clan kin of the groom confirm an alliance of kin support for each other. The husband's kin begin to prepare her wedding outfit, which consists of a large and a small white cotton robe, a wide plaited cotton belt, a pair of wraparound white buckskin boots, a white cotton shawl, a black wool dress, and a reed mat in which to carry one of her cotton blankets and belt (fig. 41). The cotton and wool to be carded, spun and woven are contributed by his kinsmen, who also provide the weavers. Completion of the wedding outfit may take several years, and if children are born to the couple, robes must also be woven for them. When the outfit is completed, the bride is dressed in the wedding outfit and escorted back to the home of her mother. There they begin or may already have begun the weaving of plaques and the grinding of cornmeal to make payment for the bridal outfit. As the day of payment nears, piki must be made, sheep slaughtered and other foods prepared. When all is ready, the bride's kinsmen carry the offerings to the house of the groom's mother.

The public acknowledgment that the clans of the bride and groom have met all their commitments to each other and are now bound into supportive kin ties takes place when the bride appears in the plaza dressed in her bridal outfit. This event takes place at the final round of the next Niman Kachina Dance, the last masked ceremony in the ritual year.

Marriage rituals are both individual and clan commitments. They signify supportive clan alliances which cut across the class status structure of clans. In addition to providing family and group continuity, the marriage rituals function as mechanisms for establishing interclan alliances.

The prime clan household husbands and manages the resources of the clan. It must sustain its membership to ensure support for meeting its commitments. It must concurrently contain

*Tomorrow is the feast day for the official spinning for the cotton to be used for Louise's wedding robe. Many people have come to Oraibi for the event, and there were more Hotevilla women than had ever before been seen in the pueblo. Several sheep have been slaughtered, and nearly every woman in Oraibi is baking piki. There is an air of hustle and bustle and pleasant activity...*

Mischa Titiev
*The Hopi Indians of Old Oraibi*
December 4, 1933

aggressive dispositions of its own group and ward off aggressions upon it from other groups. Aggressions, whether internal or external, are generated not so much by the human capacity for behaving obnoxiously as by the natural circumstances of the environment. How does one ward off the assaults of sandstorm violence, of summer flood, of drought? How does one moderate the human anxieties stirred up by these natural occurrences? In the broadest sense, by maintaining the Hopi way. The Hopi way is not so much a philosophical generalization as an ongoing attentiveness to the responsibilities of life learned in the household of one's clan. But as clan survival is dependent upon the cooperative support of its members, so community survival is dependent upon the clans' support in the performance of ceremony. This cooperative clan activity reaffirms to the community as a whole that "we, the Hopi are surviving."

Fig. 41. Second Mesa Hopi bride returning to her mother's home from groom's home dressed in her newly woven black dress and two white robes carrying her reed "suitcase" which is wrapped around the rain sash and white robe. 1930s. Courtesy of the Museum of Northern Arizona.

Fig. 42. Ceramic jars decorated with Polik Mana Kachinas and metal wash buckets filled with payment for bridal outfit—finely ground cornmeal. Photographed by J. H. Bratley, ca. 1902. Courtesy of the Denver Museum of Natural History, Crane Collection BR61-228.

# Societies

Although theoretically each cermony of the Hopi is owned by a particular clan, and is its warranty for place and entitlements in the community, there has developed, especially with the elaboration of ceremony, a need for participatory support beyond the human resources of a single clan group. In addition, there are situations in which a clan has died out or has been incapacitated to such an extent that it cannot maintain a ceremonial responsibility. Ceremonial responsibility may be transferred to a related clan or in some instances to another clan. The nature of these transfers is not wholly clear and variations undoubtedly occur from village to village. At Shongopavi it has been reported that when a clan is unable to maintain its ceremonies, ownership reverts to the Bear Clan head, who in his role as *kikmongwi* (village father) reassigns the ceremony. Whatever the procedure, the responsibility for a particular ceremony has come to require inter-clan participation for performance and continuity.

The most widespread of all Hopi ceremonial activities is that of the kachina cult. Even in those communities, such as at Kyakotsmovi and Upper Moencopi, where all other ceremony has been abandoned or lost, the kachina cult thrives. Both boys and girls are initiated. Although the kachina ritual and dancing activities are largely carried out by men, the men are dependent upon the support system provided by women to sustain their activities. The kachinas, as Eggan (1950:91) noted, "are thought of as generalized ancestors who return with clouds and rain to help the community." A significant aspect of the kachina performances is the song, which is weighted with instruction. Song not only serves as the communication link with the generalized ancestors with respect to bringing clouds and rain, but it also expresses the cumulative experience of the Hopi past—reminding the people of today that care for and use of their land and water, even now as in ancestral times, is the only surety for the future. This is an extreme simplification of the highly complex kachina cult.

Upon initiation into the kachina cult, the Hopi boy and girl become participants in kachina activities rather than only recipients of the gifts and instruction provided by the kachinas. The boys are eligible to dance in the masked dances. The girls prepare the special foods and take part in the social support system which makes the elaborate performances possible. Upon adult initiation they become full participants in the ceremonies of the societies to which they belong and become eligible to participate in the winter solstice ceremony, Soyal *(Soyalangwu).*

The Soyal is one of the less ostentatious of Hopi ceremonies, and because of this, perhaps the most impressive. In many respects it is the awakening of the Hopi year. Prayer sticks *(paavaho)*, symbolizing the best thoughts of the Hopi men, are made and distributed to the entire community. The calendar of the new ceremonial year is planned and major undertakings determined and assigned. It is the preface to a new agricultural year and introduces the return of the kachinas to the villages.

Although some ceremonies are performed in part at or near the clan house of the clan associated with the ceremony, most ceremonies are attached to a particular kiva. A kiva is a place (an underground ceremonial room) but it also designates a group—the men who customarily use it for their ceremonies.

Most ceremonies have both private or secret expressions in which only those associated with them participate, and public expressions performed for the community as a whole, purportedly for all people everywhere.

In those communities where the ceremonial structure has been maintained, boys and girls who have been initiated into the kachina cult have taken but a first step in the initiation into Hopi life. The kachina initiation involves the selection of a "ceremonial father" and a "ceremonial mother" by the family of the initiate from a clan other than that of the initiate. This assignment carries with it an extended involvement with the community and and a whole new set of kinship relations, using the same terms of kinship as learned in the natal household. The "ceremonial parent" becomes an in-lieu parent for passage from childhood and youth to adulthood. Initiation is not a generalized entry into the community, but a step toward a specific position in it. The young person will be instructed, counseled and supported in preparation for membership in the ceremonial society or societies of the "ceremonial parent." There is a preparation period of several years after kachina initiation before initiation into a society as an adult. The ceremonial societies cut across the clan-phratry system into which individuals are born, and are attached to particular kiva groups. The four major men's societies are Wuwutcim (*Wuuwutsim*), Tao (*Taatawkya*), Ahl (*Aala'ytaqa*) and Kwan (*Kwaani'ytaqa*). These societies hold annual ceremonies in November. In the years when initiation takes place, they participate jointly in the initiation ceremonies. The women's societies are Marau (*Marawu*), Oaqöl (*Owaqöl*) and Lakon (*Lalkontu*).

In addition to the major societies discussed, there are other societies to which a person may belong, such as the Snake and

Fig. 43. *Lalkontu* (Basket Dancers), Walpi, First Mesa. Photographed by Joseph Mora, 1904-1906. Courtesy of John R. Wilson.

Fig. 44. Flute Ceremony. Mishongnovi, Second Mesa, photographed by A. C. Vroman. Note the cornmeal clouds on the ground. Courtesy of the Los Angeles County Museum of Natural History V-578.

Antelope or Blue and Gray Flute societies. Membership in these may result from the influences of parents or "ceremonial parents," from having been cured by the society from a particular malady, or for other reasons. These societies are interclan in membership, although they may be under the control or in the custody of a particular clan. Upon initiation into one of the major societies the Hopi individual is recognized as an adult, having identity both as a clan member in the clan to which he was born and as a member of an interclan society of the community at large. Here again we see the processes of separation and integration at work as we have in the village clusters, the clans, lineages and households.

## Tribal Council

A twentieth century addition to Hopi social organization came about under the Indian Reorganization Act of 1934. Controversy and often acrimonious argument both preceded and followed the formation of a Hopi Tribal Council, which was approved by the Commissioner of Indian Affairs in December of 1936. The late Oliver LaFarge, distinguished author and anthropologist, had been asked by Commissioner Collier to assist the Hopi in the development of a tribal constitution and council organization. LaFarge undertook the task with reservations. As the model for such a council was a form alien to Hopi, many of the people found it antithetical to their perceptions of self-government. LaFarge recognized that Hopi social organization had a greater depth than was readily apparent and that there was inadequate knowledge of its structure and function. He also recognized that a number of Hopi people had become disassociated from the older social order through the breakup of Old Oraibi, through affiliations with various missionary groups and through expanding experiences in the broader society. LaFarge saw two dangers to the successful operation of a Hopi tribal government: one, a forcing of the issue rather than allowing for developmental process, and another, the tendency to view Hopi society in simplistic terms such as "Hostiles" and "Friendlies," which emerged during the Oraibi split. His fears were well founded. The Tribal Council became inoperative, and was recognized as such by the Hopi Agency Superintendent in 1943. The common explanation by agency employees from that time until the early fifties was, "The Hopis are not ready for self-government."

In the 1950s a renewed effort was made and the present Hopi Tribal Council resulted. The old terms "Hostiles" and "Friendlies" fell into disuse and were replaced by equally unfortunate terms, "Traditionals" and "Progressives." In both instances the implication was opposition or cooperation with respect to government, education, health care and change in general. Such terms have been used by the Hopi and outsiders alike both in derogation and in approval of individuals and groups. Actually there is no such clear-cut dichotomy in Hopi society. A greater or lesser amount of schooling, of religious or spiritual commitment, of professional competence or business acumen—the implications of these variables do not fit within the dichotomy, and such categorization of Hopi individuals or communities does not bear up under objective inquiry. The placing of individuals and communities in oppositional, competitive relationships by this fallacious dichotomy has been an obstacle to the emergence of a representative tribal organization. It has provoked alienations and antagonisms which detract from the efforts of many Hopi of goodwill seeking to resolve and accommodate to the wide diversity of views, understandings and experiences contained within Hopi society.

The effectiveness of the Hopi Tribal Council would appear to depend upon lessening its dependence upon non-Hopi authorities and resources, and increasing conviction among the Hopi people that it serves them rather than the special interests of outsiders. The fit of this added social structure with the long-established social order remains to be seen.

# Conclusion

In this review of Hopi social and ceremonial organization an attempt has been made to look at those elements of social structure through which Hopi society operates to maintain itself and an elaborate ceremonial drama. On all levels we have noted the processes of complementary separation and integration in maintaining a lifeway strong in its survival capacity and rich in its creativity—a society which has developed strategies for coping with the savage violence of its natural environment but which remains creative in its response to its awesome beauty. As it is pressed hard in its wits and energies to seek out land to cultivate, it is also pressed hard to preserve the communities, the clans, the households and the integrity of its people. As a Hopi man of insight once said to me, "It's good to be a Hopi but it's hard work to be a Hopi."

John Connelly
*Professor Emeritus*
*San Francisco State University*

# Contemporary Hopi Crafts: Basketry, Textiles, Pottery, Kachinas

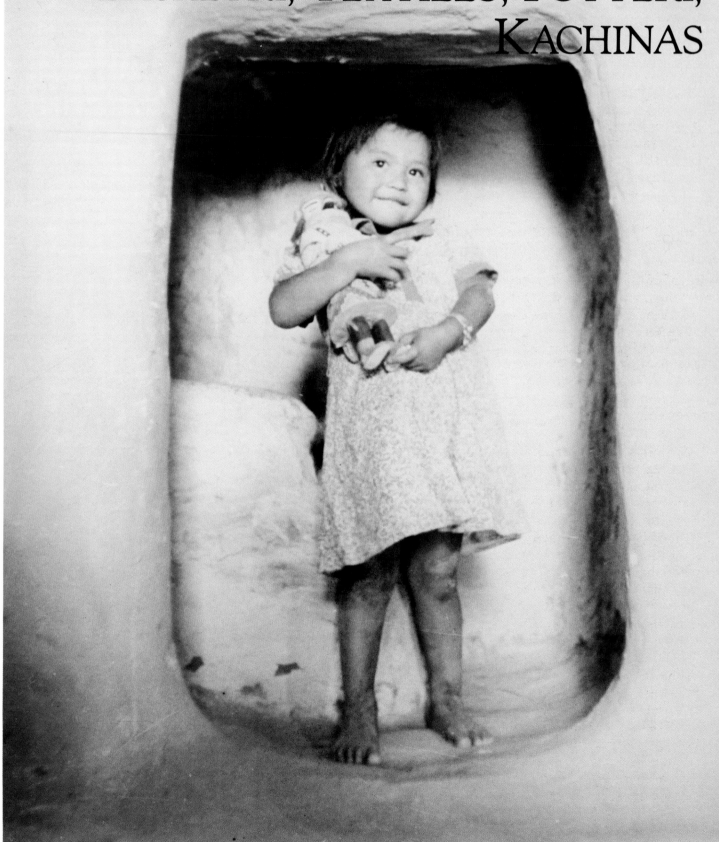

# by Clara Lee Tanner
# and John F. Tanner

Hopi Indians have preserved more of their native arts and crafts than any other Southwestern Puebloans. Among crafts still basically Hopi as inherited from their ancestors, the Anasazi, and as produced today, are baskets, textiles, pottery and kachinas ( *katsinam*). Silverwork is, of course, a late non-Indian expression. Quite naturally the older crafts have responded to both internal tribal change and to outside contact with Spaniards and Anglo-Americans. With substitutions for native items through contact, particularly in the later nineteenth century, some crafts were on the verge of dying out. However, interest on the part of the white man kept them alive to the point that native materials, technologies, forms and styles of decoration were never forgotten by the Hopi. Through the years the development of discernment and critical appreciation by the outsider has encouraged higher aesthetic qualities on the part of the Indian creators of these crafts.

## Basketry

A long tradition of basket weaving is evident in the Hopi villages today. The three basic technologies—plaiting, wicker and coiling—have prehistoric roots as do basic forms such as trays, bowls and jars. Designs were generally geometric; rarely were life forms portrayed. Observable color was basically limited to black and natural with some use of red, although it is quite likely that the ancients used other colors which time and the elements have destroyed.

This was the Hopi inheritance from the ancient past. What these Puebloans produced in the years between the Spanish Conquest in 1540 and the middle of the nineteenth century is not well known. However, historic information indicates that even after 1850 there was considerable production. During the second half of the 1880s commercial pots and pans began to appear among the Hopi, but, interestingly, by 1900 these conveniences had not completely displaced the native basketry containers.

Basketry styles in the first half of the twentieth century reflect two basic trends. First there has been a continuation of some traditional styles such as the piki ( *piiki*) tray and wedding basket, plus a limited production of baskets used for varied purposes ritually or about the home. Second, there has been the growing

Fig. 45. Hopi child with kachina tihu. Photographed by Harold Kellog, 1938. Courtesy of the Museum of New Mexico, Santa Fe 77536.

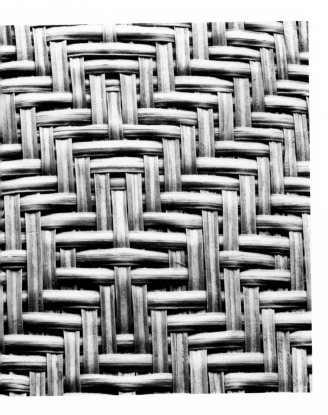

Fig. 46. Detail of twill plaiting on a yucca sifter.

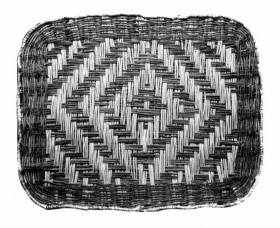

Fig. 47. Piki tray. The center of the tray is plaited and the edges are in wicker weave. No. 178.

influence of a buying public, a trend which began before the end of the 1800s and became magnified significantly after the 1950s. Public exhibitions have been very influential in the rise in quality of Hopi basketry. For example, the annual Hopi Arts and Crafts Show at the Museum of Northern Arizona in Flagstaff, which began in the early 1930s, has been directly responsible for the rise to national and international prominence of many Hopi artists and craftsmen.

Plaiting has long been used by the Hopi for the production of utility pieces such as the sifter basket. For this technique, yucca leaves are gathered and either woven green or bleached dead white. With commercialization, a greater use of both colors has become popular. Rarely, the flexible yucca elements are dyed with either native or aniline dyes. Yucca leaves are prepared by splitting to the size of the finished element, with width depending upon the specific use a woman has in mind. Whether strips are narrow, wide or medium, a good basket utilizes elements that are regular and even.

In the plain-plaiting technique, single, cut elements are crossed at right angles in an over-one-under-one rhythm. Hopi twill plaiting is an alternation of single elements in an over-two-under-two, or over-three-under-three, or other rhythm. Plain plaiting produces no pattern, while twill plaiting is productive of geometric designs which can be relatively simple or fairly complex. Most patterns in this technique are in the weave itself, although they are often made more obvious through the added manipulation of varicolored elements. Design units in plaited basketry are angular because of the right angle crossing of elements; they are large because of the width of weaving materials; and the variety is generally limited to lines, zigzags, diamonds and squares.

Forms in plaited weaves were more varied in the past than they are today. For example, jars or bottles, mats, baby cradle hoods, straps or belts, pottery rings or rests, and bowl-like forms, some with square bottoms, were produced. Today twill plaiting is used in the round tray or shallow bowl with a heavy wooden ring at the rim, and for the center of the piki tray. These two pieces are made and used in all villages on all three mesas.

One detail of interest in the plaited bowl is the rim. The weaver brings the elements up and over the wooden ring at the top, sews them in place on the outside, and cuts off the ends to less than one inch. Jemez Pueblo plaited trays can be distinguished from those made by Hopi, as they are deeper, the rim fringe is longer, and, in the weaving process, two elements instead of one are carried along simultaneously.

Wicker baskets are made only in Moenkopi (*Munqapi*) and the Third Mesa villages: Oraibi (*Orayvi*), Hotevilla (*Ho'atvela*) and Bakavi (*Paaqavi*). Hopi wicker baskets are unique, for no other examples of the same weave anywhere in the United States have surpassed these in design variety, color and complexity. Wicker baskets are started with three, four, or more bundles of stiff elements, usually sumac or wild currant twigs, which are

wrapped, placed close together and crossed at right angles by equal numbers of wrapped bundles. At the ends of the wrapped sections the multiple rods are splayed out to act as the warps. Wefts, usually of rabbit brush, are woven over and under the warps.

Since the wefts carry the design, they are dyed with vegetal and aniline dyes, plus some mineral mordants. Vegetable-dyed weft elements are dipped in the dye bath, and the color is set by smoking them over wool. There is a wide range in colors for both vegetal and aniline dyes, including reds, greens (these two were very popular about 1900), purples, yellows, orange, blues, black and white. Some of the sources of vegetable dyes and their resultant colors include alder bark, sumac berries and cockscomb flowers for red; saffron flowers for orange and yellow; a grass, *Thelesperma* sp., for red-brown; purple corn for purple; larkspur for light blue; navy bean and sunflower seed for black and blue; and blue and yellow dyes mixed for green.

Forms in wicker weave include a plaque, a round or oval bowl, a rectangular and flat piki tray, and a deeper form resembling a wastebasket for the white man. The centers of piki trays have plaited design in the light and dark brown of split sumac rods, while the borders are plain brown. Center patterns are comparable to those in the plaited tray, including a variety of arrangements of diagonals, zigzags, diamonds and triangles. To finish a wicker basket the warps are alternately cut off or bent and sewn in place, usually with black-dyed yucca.

Fig. 48. Chief Tewaquaptewa's wife making a wicker basket, Oraibi, Third Mesa. Photographed by E. B. Sayles, 1930-1940. Courtesy of the Arizona State Museum 24594.

Fig. 49. Coiled plaque with Hahai-i Wu-uti Kachina. No. 113.

In addition to a variety of curvilinear and linear geometric designs, the Hopi apply a variety of representational patterns to their wicker baskets. Birds, especially eagles, masks of kachinas or the full kachina figure, especially Crow Mother, Mudhead Kachinas, maidens with whorled hair, and butterflies are common subjects.

Seldom woven in recent years but often in significant collections of Hopi pieces is the peach basket. Contrary to all other work in this craft, peach baskets are made by the men. Whole sumac rods are used for the warp. The rectangular shape is maintained by the placement of a heavy U-shaped wooden rod at each end. The weave is coarse; no design normally appears on the walls or bases of this form.

Coiled basketry is woven by the Hopi in the Second Mesa villages of Mishongnovi (*Musangnuvi*), Shipaulovi (*Supawlavi*) and Shongopavi (*Songoopavi*). Through the years changes in technique have centered in decrease of coil size, finer stitching and more elaborate and sophisticated patterning. At the turn of the century, each coil was often an inch in width; today there are two or more coils to the inch. In both earlier and recent pieces there is an average of fourteen stitches to the inch.

Forms in Hopi coiled baskets are generally similar to those in wicker, except for the addition of coiled jars. Plaques are flatter, since they lack the hump common to the wicker pieces. More frequently, the coiled bowl has a slightly incurving rim in contrast to the dominantly straight-sided wicker piece.

Yucca is the principal material used in Hopi coiled baskets, often shredded for the large round foundation, and carefully cut for the sewing material. Grasses such as galleta may be substituted for the yucca foundation. The coils are sewn in a counterclockwise direction with noninterlocking stitches. Yucca leaves are bleached white for background wefts and dyed a soft reddish brown or red, black and yellow for the designs.

Designs in coiled basketry are formed by introducing the colored element under several stitches before it becomes active in the sewing. When its part in the design is terminated, then the element is cut off or buried under further stitching until again needed. The rim is always finished in the same stitch used in making the basket; however, the rim color may vary considerably from the design area. For example, the design may terminate one coil before the rim, and the terminal rim coil is simply all black or all white. In other instances, the design is completed in the rim coil. For example, if there is a cloud pattern, the top of the colored cloud may be part of the rim coil.

Designs include both geometric and life forms. Geometrics include lines and bands, zigzags, triangles and diamonds, the latter two often with stepped borders in a contrasting color. Life motifs vary from relatively simple floral patterns to masks, kachinas, birds, deer, sun symbols and turtles. In recent years some Hopi women have produced raised representations of a frog or turtle on the bottom of a plaque or shallow bowl.

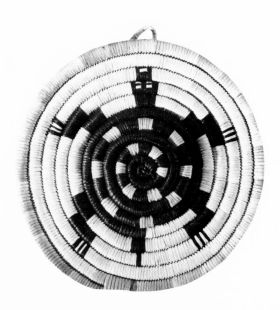

Fig. 50. Coiled plaque with turtle. No. 112.

Although coiled baskets are usually made exclusively on Second Mesa, and wicker pieces on Third Mesa, plaited trays, peach baskets and piki trays may be produced on any of the Mesas. The latter situation probably prevailed in earlier years for the three types of basketry, especially as each woman produced all of the baskets used by her family.

A few basketry uses are unique. Formerly a bride wove a large coiled basket decorated in a black and green design on a white ground for her groom. Some examples have been as large as two feet to three feet in diameter. The groom kept this all his life, and it was buried with him, for tradition indicated that this basket was necessary for his passage to the next world. Today it is common for a dozen or more baskets to be made for exchange between the families of the married couple.

Coiled and wicker plaques heaped with cornmeal or piki are carried in ceremonial processions. At the *Lalkontu*, the woman's society dance, they are given away after the performance. Small coiled baskets, about three inches in diameter are given to newborn babies by the kachinas. Comparable plaques were also presented to the eagles captured by the Hopi and kept until *Niman* for their feathers.

Like so many other craft arts, Hopi basketry has become highly commercialized. As a matter of fact, had this trend not developed, it is quite likely that there would be very little of this craft today. Of all Southwestern tribes, the Hopi are second only to the Papago in quantity production, but their baskets rank with the best in quality.

Fig. 51. Groom's coiled plaque. No. 177.

# Textiles

The earliest evidence of textile production in the American Southwest dates to the time of the ancient hunter-gatherers. Some six or eight thousand years ago these semisedentary people made twined rabbit fur blankets, and belts and bands of various native fibers. More than 1400 years ago, there is evidence of beautifully patterned belts and bands of native fibers such as yucca. About A.D. 700 cotton and the loom were introduced, probably from the south. This allowed the production of many different types of garments. It was now possible to weave pieces such as shirts, breech cloths, dresses, body and shoulder blankets and belts. Although the majority of items were made in plain weave, some were in fancy weaves such as twills, tapestry, slit tapestry, gauze and weft float, and some pieces were decorated with brocading and embroidery.

These early fabrics were ornamented with a variety of designs, some in the weave itself, some in woven color, and some painted on the finished piece of cloth. The earliest patterns were geometric because they were produced by the weave. This angular style carried over into other decorative techniques, even into the motifs which were painted on after the fabrics were woven. Black was the dominant color used for cloth design, with red and brown next in prominence, and with limited amounts of green, blue and yellow. Designs in these prehistoric fabrics vary from simple stripes and bands to checkers, stepped motifs, frets, zigzags, triangles and meanders. Patterns might be arranged over the entire surface of all types of clothing, or they might be limited either to borders of a blanket or to the center of a large or smaller piece. Some of the more elaborate weaves, such as twining, slit tapestry, gauze and weft-wrapped, and some forms such as the cord apron, did not survive. However, belts and headbands, braided sashes and rectangular or square products of the loom have persisted to this day.

The Hopi Indians continued to cultivate cotton, *Gossypium hopi*, during the historic period. A few men raised it into the 1930s in order to have a supply for ceremonial garments. Nonetheless, by the turn of the century many elements of American culture had been introduced which would radically change the character of some Hopi weaving. Since cotton batting was available at trading posts by 1890, some weavers began substituting it, first for warps and later for the entire fabric. Other Hopi totally substituted a coarse heavy cotton cord for native plain cloth. When the Hopi acquired sheep from Spanish missionaries, wool began to supplant cotton, particularly for their nonritual garments. Carders, also from the Spaniards, were used for both wool and cotton. Commercial wool yarn, first available in Hopi country about 1880, from eastern manufacturers, became popular for use in embroidery and brocading. Although the Hopi, encouraged by the Museum of Northern Arizona, continued to produce some of their own colors from native plants, the introduction of aniline dyes by traders led to some changes in the character of Hopi design. Commercial fabrics replaced practically all everyday handwoven clothing.

Hopi textiles have been dominated by the natural wool colors of white, brown and brown-black. Indigo-dyed blue, reds, green, orange and real black were produced from natural dyes. Most native cotton was plain white or cream, but a fair amount of color, especially red, green and black, was added in embroidered and brocaded patterns. Belts and bands were dominantly red or white, with some touches of black and more limited use of other colors.

Designs in historic Hopi fabrics were by no means as varied as they were in the cloth of prehistoric times, particularly in terms of allover elaboration of pattern. Simple bands predominated in wool blankets, with less use of plaids in other pieces. Wide bands of plain red and dark blue were also fairly popular in cotton shoulder blankets.

Hopi men are the weavers for all fabrics except the rabbit fur blanket. This situation apparently has prehistoric roots, for archaeologists have found evidences of loom anchors in the kiva, an underground ceremonial chamber used almost exclusively by men. Today the upright loom is set up close to the kiva wall, or sometimes in a room of the man's house. The top loom bar is suspended from ceiling beams by ropes, while the bottom bar

Fig. 52. Hopi man weaving woman's black dress. Photographed by J. H. Bratley, ca. 1902. Courtesy of the Denver Museum of Natural History, Crane Collection BR61-226.

is attached to a beam anchored to the floor. A tension bar is fastened to the top loom bar and the warp is secured to both the top and bottom loom beams.

Warps are strung and stabilized on these bars in the following manner. Two small poles have their ends set in holes in the wall, the other ends in loom blocks. The poles rest about six inches above the ground level. A thread is tied close to one end of one pole, and the ball of yarn is then thrown back and forth over both poles, crossing in the center and thus forming a figure eight in the warps. The distance between poles determines the fabric length; the number and arrangement of warps establish the fabric width.

Warps are made stationary in relation to each other and strong ends for the fabric are produced by twining warps together over the outer edge of each pole. If it is desired to have warps closer together for a finer fabric, the twist between every two warps is limited to one. If the weaving is to be coarser, there may be two or three twists between warps. This twining serves another purpose, for it makes possible the lashing of warps to a second set of poles, one at each end, thus allowing the poles about which the original warping was done to be removed. The new top pole is attached to the tension bar, which allows the weaver to make his warps taut or to lower them as he weaves. The new bottom pole is secured to the stationary bar on the floor.

For plain weave a long, thin stick called a heddle is loosely attached with cord so as to bring forward alternate warp threads; another long stick is inserted between warps so as to do the same to alternating threads. For twill weaves, different alternations are set up with heddle and heald rods. The batten stick, inserted between the warps and turned on its face, creates an opening or shed for the passage of wefts. For tapestry weaves a batten or a wooden comb is used to beat down the wefts to conceal warps.

Another form of upright loom is strung and manipulated like the regular loom to produce a woven belt. This belt, or waist, loom, which creates a narrower and much longer piece, is strung with continuous warps in tubular form. This means that since the warps do not cross in figure eight fashion the belt will be twice the length of the loom. Since there is no frame, one loom end is fastened to a projection on the wall and the other end is secured about the waist of the weaver. To apply tension, the weaver simply leans back. This loom can also be placed in an upright position. In this type the warps are moved around the end bars or "rollers" in order to keep them always directly in front of the weaver.

Fig. 53. Kuwan Heheya Kachina Line Dance, Walpi, First Mesa. Photographed by Joseph Mora, 1904-1906. Courtesy of John R. Wilson.

When stringing warps for belts, various colors, primarily red, black, green and white, are placed on the rollers in a pre-conceived order. During the weaving process these are "floated," or brought forward by the wefts to create pattern in the warps. Garters and hair ties are made of wool in the same warp float weave as the belts, using red and green or white and red, or all three colors. Indigo blue was sometimes substituted for the green. These small pieces run from about fifteen to twenty inches in length and are slightly over one inch in width. Often they have no more than a green or white stripe or some very simple geometric theme repeated down the center.

During later historic years Hopi men employed a variety of weaves. Plain weave, often called basket weave, is a simple over-one-under-one alternation. Both warps and wefts are exposed in the finished product. Plain tapestry weave involves essentially the same alternation of wefts over warps, with the former battened down to conceal the latter. There is a variety of tapestry weaves called twills. These involve such alternations as over-two-under-one, over-two (or three)-under-two (or three) or over-three-under-one. Each weave combination produces a different pattern of diagonal lines, zigzags or diamonds.

A favorite Hopi decorative technique, brocading, is done during the weaving process by the introduction of a thread which is not involved with the structural elements of the cloth. This strictly decorative thread is introduced along with the white weft at points controlled by the weaver to create design. The Hopi also use embroidery, a technique in which colored threads are applied to the white fabric after it has been completed.

One of the most interesting products of the Hopi weaver is the braided sash. Made by the father of the bridegroom for the bride, the sash is produced on a small horizontal loom which is set up in a fashion similar to that of the belt loom. During the braiding process the threads are held in position with long, slender rods. Braiding is continued until a three-foot unwoven section remains: here the threads are cut to make a fringe at each end. The long fringes are symbolic of rain; hence this sash is often referred to as a rain sash.

Rabbit fur robes, woven by women, are made with strips of rabbit hide fastened together in one long piece and twisted or wound about a wool cord. A simple loom frame is set up with an upper horizontal pole suspended from a ceiling beam and a lower horizontal pole fastened to the floor. The fur cord is "strung," or looped continuously over top and bottom bars, thus forming the warps. The weaver now twines the strips together with a double wool yarn at intervals of several inches. This type of weaving is sometimes called finger weaving.

It is interesting to note that the Spaniards introduced both knitting needles and crochet hooks to the Pueblo Indians. Knitting became popular among the Hopi for the production of footless stockings twelve to fourteen inches long. These were held in position with red garters. They were made of dark blue or black aniline-dyed or white wool yarn, usually commercial.

Fig. 54. Detail of braiding on rain sash. No. 172.

Fig. 55. Hopi women making rabbit skin blanket, Mishongnovi, Second Mesa. Photographed by El-wood Harvey Allcutt, October, 1899. Courtesy of the Treganza Anthropology Museum, San Francisco State University 77.

A ridge characterized some of these pieces at the top and bottom. In some instances, a cable stitch created a curving band down the length of each stocking.

Each garment is woven in a specific weave and uses a specific type of material. Usually, ceremonial objects, including kilts, the woman's wedding dress and other ceremonial pieces, are produced in plain weave, in cotton. Some kilts are of wool, in diagonal twill, as are some shirts and breechcloths. Plain blankets for boys, ceremonial sashes, and baby blankets are woven of wool in plain weave.

Ceremonial sashes are brocaded in commercial wool yarn, usually in red, green and black. These wide plain-woven sashes are made in two identical pieces, each measuring about forty inches or more in length and about eleven inches in width. Approximately one-third to one-half of each piece is brocaded in three major horizontal decorative bands. At the top and bottom are deeper or more flattened zigzags made up of small white triangles on a black background. In the center, and on a green ground, are, usually, three sets of paired vertical lines with hooked ends and two large red and white diamonds.

When men's shirts were still being made they were woven of cotton or wool in plain weave and then embroidered. It is probable that the embroidered white shirts were meant more for ceremonial occasions, for they are often most lavish in appearance. Some simpler, plain indigo blue or black wool shirts were made of three pieces of diagonal twill sewn together.

Plain tapestry weave, using wool, is employed to make bed blankets and some of the general everyday wearing blankets. Some of the bed blankets are woven thicker and heavier to serve as rugs. For many years the decoration of blankets remained relatively simple, with edge to edge stripes and bands the most typical designs. Baby blankets and those for small children were ornamented with edge to edge stripes and narrow bands, usually in dark blue and black. With increase in size, there was generally an increase in complexity of design and colors, but they were usually always edge to edge in pattern arrangement.

The central section of the maiden's shawl used in ceremonies is made of white wool or cotton in a diagonal-twill weave, while the borders are in diamond twill. They are typically woven with broad red and dark blue, or sometimes black bands at top and bottom, but always two or three thin white lines are left in one or both of the colored bands. This detail is evidenced in examples from at least 1870 to the present.

The central section of the woman's dark wool blanket dress was woven in diagonal twill in black or dark brown, while the two wide borders were in dark blue diamond twill. These two subtly woven sections are marked by red and green yarn lines at their junctions. This garment was a single, wide piece worn under the left arm, caught up over the right arm, and belted with a red belt. Originally worn as an everyday dress, it later became a ritual garment and is worn today only on ceremonial occasions.

A Hopi man weaves two plain white blankets for the girl his son is to marry. One is worn about her shoulders during parts of the wedding rite. She is to keep this blanket for the rest of her life and upon her death it is to be buried with her. Within a year after her marriage, she may embroider a section along the top and bottom borders and wear this robe on ritual occasions. Some of the motifs used in the borders are diamonds, stepped clouds with dripping rain, flowers and butterflies. Yellow, red, blue and sometimes orange are used in the designs within the diamonds, while green and black dominate the rest of the border.

Boys' plaid blankets are generally small in size and are of plain weave in brown and white wool. On the other hand, the man's wool blanket is larger, black and white, and woven in all-over diamond twill, or with diamond twill borders and a diagonal twill center, or in a herringbone and diagonal twill combination.

Indeed, Hopi weaving has had a long and illustrious history. Although sheep, new yarns, aniline dyes and new techniques and materials brought through historic contacts have been absorbed by the Hopi, they still have maintained many traditional styles, forms and functions. Hundreds of years of symbolism in ritual use coupled with the beauty of traditional design ideals ensure that the Hopi will not neglect continuities in textile production.

Fig. 56. Brocaded ceremonial sash. No. 164.

Fig. 57. Detail of woman's black wool dress. No. 169.

# Pottery

The earliest Anasazi pottery was made several centuries after the opening of the Christian Era and was greatly influenced by basket forms and decoration. Indeed, weave impressions on vessel fragments indicate that some of the first pieces were molded inside baskets. Painted designs on these early wares were crudely executed and featured the angularity of basketry patterns.

Through the centuries, descendant Pueblo dwellers developed regional styles. For some years after initial Spanish contact, both decorated and undecorated pottery continued to be produced in all Hopi pueblos. In time, decorated wares were made solely on First Mesa, although utility pieces such as storage and cooking jars continued to be made in other villages, especially Hotevilla.

Early historic Hopi wares were characterized by a predominance of heavy-walled, sloppily painted and simply designed pieces. Geometric decorations were in black or brown on yellow or in polychromes. Some of the designs reflect a probable Rio Grande influence, particularly from the Tewa people, who settled Hano about 1700. Such designs include leaflike patterns, the split feather, key motifs, and drawn-out triangles with curved sides.

At the turn of the century three distinctive wares were made. Polacca Polychrome was decorated largely in geometrics on an almost white slip which crazed upon firing. Walpi Polychrome was an unslipped ware decorated in red and black on the natural orange-yellow ground with a great variety of geometric and life designs. The third style, Sikyatki Polychrome, was one of the most famous Hopi wares. It was first produced during the fifteenth century, and later revived by Nampeyo, a Tewa woman living at Hano. She was influenced by designs from sherds her husband, Lesou, brought from prehistoric Sikyatki, excavated under the direction of archaeologist J. Walter Fewkes.

Sikyatki wares were either brown-on-yellow or polychrome with black and red designs on a buff or yellowish ground. Both geometric and life designs were painted in the center bottom of low shallow bowls with incurved rims or on the flat shoulders of jars without necks. Design elements varied from plain or stepped triangles, squares, heavy crosses, lines and bands to slightly realistic life forms including humans, kachinas, rabbits, deer, snakelike creatures, birds, doglike animals and butterflies. Highly conventionalized were snakes and birds or their feathers, wings or beaks.

Nampeyo's "revival ware" was not an exact copy of either the Sikyatki vessel forms or of its designs. The jars acquired necks and the designs often covered most of the exterior vessel wall instead of being restricted to the flat shoulder area. Bowls retained their low incurved form but the interior designs became more varied. Kachina masks and life forms, and especially stylized feathers were common motifs. Frequently asymmetrical designs were placed so as to sweep from bowl rim to center.

Although becoming blind in her later years, Nampeyo continued to make pottery. Her husband, Lesou, decorated her ves-

Fig. 58. Nampeyo firing pottery, Hano, First Mesa. Photographed by Joseph Mora, 1904–1906. Courtesy of John R. Wilson.

sels; after his death her daughter, Fannie, assumed this task. Nampeyo had shared her wealth of design tradition with her four daughters, Nellie, Fannie, Cecilia and Annie, and this family set an example for all Hopi potters in the constant production of fine ceramics. In a 1974 exhibit at the Maxwell Museum, *Seven Families in Pueblo Pottery*, the pottery of Nampeyo, her four daughters, eleven of her granddaughters, seven great-granddaughters and five great-great-granddaughters was represented.

Different traditional vessel forms of Hopi pottery reflect specific functional requirements. The two main forms made today for sale are low bowls with incurved rims, formerly for serving and eating, and jars with flat shoulders and short necks, originally for water and food storage. The only bowls which are still made and constantly used by Hopi are deep and straight walled, and are used for mixing the liquid piki dough. Every woman has several of these classic undecorated vessels as part of her basic household equipment.

The traditional Hopi canteen carried by men to their fields was usually flat on the back side, with a very small neck and two knobs or loops on the sides for suspension. Large water storage jars were made flat on one side to rest in a permanent spot in the home. Both the small spout and lugs for lifting these jars were placed low on the body toward the flat bottom. Smaller canteens and sometimes the large storage jars carry painted designs. Smaller ceramic pieces such as ladles, formerly used to scoop the contents from the bowls and jars, and rattles are infrequently produced.

The vase form was reputedly introduced to the Hopi by a white woman. This is a tall, slender, flat-bottomed, almost straight-sided, widemouthed vessel unlike any produced in the Hopi area either in prehistoric or early historic times. It is decorated in the typical Sikyatki revival style.

*The Ancient People didn't have pencils, so I learned to measure with my fingers. When I was small I would sneak a piece of clay and work where my grandmother could not see me. One day while my grandmother was sweeping, she found some of my small pieces hidden under the stove and she encouraged me to continue working.*

Daisy Hooee Nampeyo
*Seven Families in Pueblo Pottery*

Fig. 59. Ceramic canteen. No. 119.

Another little-known type of Hopi ceramics is the tile. These were made available to tourists in quantity beginning about the turn of the century at the request of trader Thomas Keam. Varying in shape from square to rectangular, diamond shaped and hexagonal, they are of classic buff or slipped red colors and decorated with geometrics or life forms similar to those used on Sikyatki-style vessels. A few forms have been developed more recently by the Hopi strictly to answer the needs of the tourist trade: candlesticks, ashtrays, match holders, boxes, small dishes and handled bowls.

Hopi pottery continues to be handmade and fired in the open. Each potter collects and prepares her own clay. The clay is soaked and kneaded, and undesirable particles are removed. Hopi usually do not add a temper (additional crushed rock or sherd fragments which facilitate evenness of shrinkage during the firing process) to their decorated ware but do add coarsely ground sandstone to clay for utility pieces. Usually the base is formed within another vessel, and large coils of clay are successively attached until the desired height is reached.

After all or nearly all of the coils have been added, surfaces are scraped with a gourd rind to build out and thin the rounding wall. A final smoothing of the surface with a piece of sandstone completes those vessels which are not to be decorated. Indeed, many Hopi pots are not slipped (a thin layer of colored clay), for the body clay itself turns a pleasing yellowish-orange or buff color when fired. However, some vessels with a deep red and all vessels with a dead white background are first slipped with these colored clays and then polished with a stone. The most common paint combinations used for decoration include black applied to buff or yellow wares, black and red on buff, black and white on red, or black and red on white.

Slips and paints are derived from several sources. White is usually a kaolin clay; red is derived from ochres; black is made by mixing boiled tansy mustard stems with hematite. Painting is the major decorative technique, although there is occasional texturing of the surface with a stick to create triangular impressions. A few potters have begun to model the surface or to insert turquoise on their finished vessels.

Firing is the most critical step of the pottery-making process. A woman builds a fire of wood and sheep manure, allows it to burn down, then lays a second one with wood, manure and coal. A platform is constructed over this fire with broken pottery, sandstone slabs, or sometimes tin. Pots are stacked upside down on this surface, covered with more broken pottery and tin and finally with a layer of sheep dung and coal, and then the fire is reignited. When the fire burns down, the pots are left in the ashes for eight or nine hours or sometimes overnight. This cooling process allows the clay walls to adjust slowly to the change in temperature and prevents cracking which might occur if vessels thus fired were suddenly pulled into the open.

Fig. 60. Firing of Rosetta Huma's pots with tin covers and dung fuel, First Mesa, Sichomovi. Photographed by Helga Teiwes. Courtesy of the Arizona State Museum, University of Arizona 37674.

In the past when the Hopi made pottery for everyday use, each woman produced what her family needed. Before the turn of the century, contacts with Anglo-Americans brought metal and other household utensils to the Indians, and thus Hopi women made less and less pottery for themselves and sold most of what they produced to tourists. Beginning in the late 1960s and into the 1970s, a strong nationwide interest in Indian crafts developed. Individual Hopi potters began spending more time specializing in distinctive styles. Signing of pots became standard; some men produced fine wares. Exhibits, competitive shows with prize monies, and shops which featured distinctive ceramics have brought Hopi pottery and potters to international recognition.

Since about 1920, the Hano Polychrome style has dominated Hopi ceramic production. Some of the Hopi potters producing today include Dextra Quotskuyva Nampeyo, Garnet Pavatea, Grace Chapella, Priscilla Namingha Nampeyo, Rachel Namingha, Nellie Nampeyo, Beth Sakeva, Laura Tomasie, Fannie Nampeyo and her son, Thomas Polacca, Helen Naha (Feather Woman), Beatrice Naha, Joy Navasie (Frog Woman), Eunice Navasie, Sadie Adams, Ethel Youvella, Lorna Lomakima and Wallace Youvella.

One of the most sophisticated Hopi wares today has been developed by Mrs. Elizabeth White of Polacca. On a white or off-white base, she models figures in relief, such as ears of corn complete with kernels, or hunchback flute players. Other specialities include the following: Helen Naha (Feather Woman) produces textured surfaces on jar forms with triangular impressions. She also has revived the prehistoric black-on-white style characterized by interlocking geometric motifs. Wallace Youvella places stippled decoration on red-slipped jars. Joy Navasie (Frog Woman) decorates her pieces with the usual red and black de-

*I did a lot of experimenting. My mother strictly opposed my doing new designs. She always said, 'Hold to the traditional.' Well, I think that is good, but younger potters always want to change or add something to it.*

Dextra Quotskuyva Nampeyo
article by Guy and Doris Monthan
in *American Indian Art Magazine*
Autumn 1977

signs on a white slip, often using the traditional theme of two opposed birds, one on each side of a flowerlike theme. Garnet Pavatea uses birds or wings or more complex geometrics on jars decorated in the black-on-red style.

Just as Nampeyo made dramatic changes in Hopi pottery, the Hopi ceramists of the 1970s are continuing to refine form and design, develop new adaptations of design to space, and introduce new texturing, modeling, paints and other techniques to the decorative process. Today Hopi pottery is no longer characterized by village-wide styles, but by a flowering of individual creativity. Many potters now have their own distinctive styles, each representing a new avenue of expression in Hopi ceramics.

# Kachinas

Fig. 6l. Hahai-i Wu-uti Puchtihu. No. 106.

Among many other things, a kachina is a spirit being who lives for six months of the year on the San Francisco Peaks and for the other six months in Hopi villages. Some are spirits of the dead, some are Cloud People. Kachinas are also masked men who act as intermediaries between the Hopi and the gods. Kachina dolls (*tihus*) are carved representations of these beings which are given by the Pueblo performers to children during dances, particularly to little girls, partly to teach them the costumes, masks and details of some important personages, and to the women as symbols of fertility, and as "an overt prayer for supernatural association and assistance," particularly for rain, good crops and other blessings. The tihus are usually hung from the house rafters or on walls. There is also a flat, slablike doll called a puchtihu (*putstihu*), which is hung on the cradles of tiny babies to protect them from harm. The first one given is the kachina grandmother, Hahai-i Wu-uti (*Hahay'i Wuuti*).

Details of Hopi religion are known only by the ceremonial leaders. Hopi spend a lifetime gradually becoming more integrated into the secrets of both kachina and nonkachina rites. This educational process begins when children are between six and ten years of age, at which time both boys and girls are initiated into the kachina cult at Powamu (*Powamuya*) celebration in late February. From then on the boys can visit or stay in the kiva; girls or women are not normally allowed to do so except, for example, when the latter whitewash the walls before and bring food during ceremonies.

When kachinas are in the Hopi villages for six months of the year between the Powamu and Niman celebrations, their main function is to dance, pray, sing and give gifts to the children in order to bring rain and sun, and to make corn, beans and other crops grow. At Powamu, beans are force-sprouted in overheated kivas and are distributed by the kachinas to all inhabitants of the village. As many as 200 kachina dancers may appear at this opening performance, for it is a dramatic announcement of their return and presence in the village. During the next six months there is constant ceremonial activity. Each dance is accompanied by secret purificatory and supplicatory rites in the kiva. Also, throughout the kachina season public performances are presented in the open plazas. The end of the kachina season is marked in July by the "Home Dance," when each village thanks the kachinas for their help and blessings during the past growing season.

The history of the kachinas is difficult to trace, but there is some prehistoric evidence which suggests that this ceremonial system is of extreme antiquity. Too, it may have roots in Meso-american cultures. The oldest evidence of a probable kachina doll is a carved and partially painted wooden figure found in Double Butte Cave near Phoenix, Arizona, dated about the twelfth or thirteenth century. The head of this piece is shaped like a mask and the stance is stiff, with the body wrapped in a blanket in the manner of early historic carved kachina dolls. There are diagonal lines across the chest, suggestive of a bandolier, which was worn by some kachinas of historic times. Supporting the possibility that this is a "kachina" is a Hopi legend which says that these sacred spirits came from Casa Grande, a prehistoric site sixty miles to the southeast of Phoenix.

Prehistoric photographs and petroglyphs in the Southwest also depict masks and full dance figures. Many are too generalized to be identified, but there is no question that the representations are masked. In many of the late prehistoric kiva murals at Awatovi, Kuaua and Pottery Mound kachinas are frequently represented in ceremonial scenes; some of these can be identified with those of the historic Hopi. For example, at Awatovi, one figure has a round mask, half gray and half white with a large black triangle centered on the lower face, great slab ears, with crosses over all and eagle tail feathers projecting from the head. There seems no doubt that this is an Awatovi version of the Hopi *Ahöla*, the leader of the kachinas at Powamu. Not only are masks significant in relating Awatovi kachinas to those of historic times but so too are much of the dancers' dress and paraphernalia.

Representations of masks or masked personages also appear on pottery. One vessel from Awatovi has a mask similar to the kachina Kokopelmana (*Kokopöl Mana*), the female Kokopelli (*Kookopölö*). Painting of masks on pottery continued into the historic period. It is recorded that Nampeyo was still producing Hano clan symbols, including masks, in 1895, when she abandoned them for the Sikyatki-inspired designs. The Corn Maid, or Salako (*Sa'lako*) Mana, covers the entire interior of many of these early bowls.

It has been estimated that there are between 250 and 350 kachinas, but it is difficult to give an exact figure because these important personages are both discontinued and added to through the years. When Fewkes worked among the Hopi in the 1890s, he had several of these Puebloans paint all the kachinas they knew. He also asked several older men in the tribe to identify kachinas they had known in earlier years but which no longer appeared in the dances; some of these were so carefully and completely identified by the elderly Hopi that the artists could and did paint them.

Fig. 62. Ahöla Kachina carved by Jimmie Kewanwytewa, 1942. No. 30.

Each different kachina has its own individual characteristics. The mask is the most important feature. Each dancer keeps his own mask, refurbishing it before a performance. Masks of more important kachinas are kept in secret spots in the kiva, but lesser ones may be taken home by the owner and placed in a safe spot. Many of these dancers wear the same costumes, or approximately the same, each year they perform.

Kachina dolls are carved from the roots of the cottonwood tree, usually picked up as driftwood which has washed down from locations north of the villages. Many Hopi have gone to the area of Grand Falls on the Little Colorado River and collected wood which has had the bark removed as it washed over the falls. Today cottonwood root sells for very high prices. Several years ago a piece six to eight inches in diameter and a foot in length cost $20.00!

A hatchet or butcher knife is used to first rough out the doll after a section is sawed off. Then with a finer knife and wood rasp, larger details are carved. A pocket knife, or if the worker can afford it, more refined carving tools, and sandpaper are used to finish the figure. After the doll is completely formed and the headpiece and other projecting details are added (today secured with white glue, and sometimes pegs), the entire piece is given an allover wash of local white clay. Today this clay is sometimes difficult to obtain, so some Hopi men have started substituting acrylic or gesso. These commercial substitutes also assure a brighter finish to the painted doll.

Traditionally, colors used in painting kachina dolls were derived from native sources: oxides of iron, copper ores, colored clays and vegetal dyes. Later, watercolors, oil-based house paints, inks and bluing were introduced to the Hopi by white men. These were displaced by the end of the nineteenth century by tempera or opaque watercolor paints. Most of the tempera, better known as poster paints, had the great disadvantage of rubbing off. In an effort to fix the paints, experimentation was carried on with sprays—even hair sprays! This became unnecessary with the introduction of acrylics, for they satisfied all the requirements of the doll maker, giving bright, beautiful and lasting colors.

After the doll is painted, various items often have to be attached: feathers or hair for the headpiece; leather, cloth and yarn for arm, leg, foot and waist decoration; green spruce bough for a ruff about the neck; cloth for garments; and shells, tin or silver, plus beads for jewelry. Some older dolls as well as many modern ones have nothing added after they are painted. Of particular interest is the way the green bough about the neck has been changed, for real spruce dries and turns brown over time. Various Hopi doll makers have solved this problem either by carving and painting this section, by using plastic imitations, by dyeing English seaweed, or, finally by substituting short lengths of green yarn. Contacts with the outside world have brought in new materials for various accessories. For example, shells for jewelry may come from the South Pacific or Zanzibar, and mink is often used for parts of the Wolf Kachina.

Fig. 63. Sio Hemis Kachina dating from ca. 1900.
No. 152.

One of the major problems of kachina doll making in recent
years has been obtaining the proper feathers. Formerly specific
feathers of specific birds were mandatory according to the religious beliefs of the Hopi. In 1973 the United States Fish and Wild-
life Service began enforcing a law to protect all migratory birds
and this prohibited the use of feathers from these species. As an
alternative, some of these craftsmen made an effort to carve and
paint feathers.

It is interesting to note that here as in other crafts, the Hopi
never signed their products until encouraged to do so by the
white man. The first kachina doll maker to sign his carvings was
Jimmie Kewanwytewa, a Hopi who worked for the Museum of
Northern Arizona. Today, it is common practice for the majority
of these Hopi artists to sign their work.

The artistic development of the kachina doll presents an interesting story of stylistic change. Tihus made before 1890 are
either naked figures or are stiffly dressed in highly stylized gar-

Fig. 64. Wakas (Cow Kachina) carved by Jimmie
Kewanwytewa. No. 146.

ments. Some of the naked figures show the influence of the cradle
doll, particularly in the broad vertical lines painted from neck to
feet and the arms hugging the body. Hands are slightly modeled,
legs are indicated by vertical cuts into the wood and feet are mere
projections out of the lifeless limbs. On a few pre-1890 dolls garments are represented, some even with a little painted detail on
kilts and sashes. Masks and headdresses are proportionately greater in size relative to the rest of the body; in fact, some are almost
one-third to one-half the body size. The eyes, mouth, cheeks and
chin are decorated; sometimes there are head and ear additions.
In many dolls of the late nineteenth and early twentieth centuries,
kilts are simply rounded enveloping garments which hang straight
from the waist with shapeless short legs and moccasined feet
projecting below. Some lower parts of arms were freed from the
body, some hands were slightly modeled. Later, brocaded and
embroidered designs were put on garments and masks were given
more identifying features.

During the 1930s, with the Museum of Northern Arizona's
concerted effort to revive Hopi craft arts, both the buying public
and the Hopi kachina carver were influenced by its publications,
and more directly, by the annual Hopi Craftsman Show. By the
late 1930s the tihus of Jimmie Kewanwytewa were beautifully
proportioned, colors were bright, detail was excellent. Other
Hopi doll carvers were beginning to move in the same direction.

World War II curtailed white contact with the Indians and
their encouragement of Hopi craftsmen, with the result that both
production and sales dropped. Also during the war years, dolls
were made in the old tradition. But when young men returned
from the Service, exposure to new ideas resulted in changes in
many aspects of style and production of tihus. After the war, and
in response to traders' requests, a few carvers began expressing
movement in arms and legs. By the end of the 1950s, the "action
doll" had become commonplace. The old stiff stance was not
completely abandoned, however, for many carvers continue the
traditional presentation, although often with freed arms which
might even be modeled.

By the 1960s full freedom of figure was attained and most of
the best dolls were executed in action positions. Eagle dancers
might have one foot forward, one "wing" up, one down, and
the head in profile to the body. Proportions were excellent, and
acrylic paints gave a brilliance and depth to color not before realized. A great many of the carvers now modeled arms, legs or any
exposed body parts, showing form and muscle.

As there are variations in details of many of the kachinas,
identification of dolls is often a problem. Many dolls have single
characteristics representing their most important aspect—whether it be rain making, corn growing or depicting a specific animal
or plant. These features, however, may vary, for village to village
differences in details for the same kachina are commonplace. Ad-
ditionally, certain kachinas have not appeared in some villages for
a long time. If a carver produces one of these dolls, he may make
errors in costume and mask because details have been forgotten.

Because the kachina cult is such a fundamental part of the Hopi's existence, the carving and giving of the kachina tihus are an undying craft and custom. However, museums' and collectors' interests in these dolls have initiated new trends. Some changes are the inevitable result of the contact of cultures. Nevertheless, the strength and importance of the internal Hopi way in the face of western culture ensures that kachina manifestations will persist for many years to come.

Fig. 65. Mosairu (Buffalo Kachina) ca. 1963. No. 140.

Clara Lee Tanner
*Professor Emeritus of Anthropology*
*University of Arizona*

John F. Tanner
*Former Indian Arts and Crafts Dealer*

# Modern Hopi Painting

# by J. J. Brody

The first modern Hopi paintings were commissioned in about 1900. Before then, Hopi paintings were either done as part of ritual applied to the walls of kivas or to objects such as altars, or, if they were secular, placed on domestic artifacts such as pottery containers. Each type of painting had a long history but the histories were interconnected and subject matter and forms were shared. A painting on a kiva wall could be patterned as though it were a decoration applied to a pot or a textile, while the subject painted on a pottery food serving bowl could be a kachina (*katsina*) mask, a horned serpent or cloud and rain symbols. It is not easy to define mutually exclusive secular and ritual modes of painting, and in that regard painting was much like most other everyday Hopi activities.

Although certain kinds of pictures such as kiva murals and sand paintings were made for particular ritual purposes, painting for its own sake, or to document events not already incorporated into the oral or pictorial traditions of the Hopi, was virtually unknown. Thus it is possible to identify Hopi ritual paintings while recognizing that most secular pictures contained ritual references. Testimony as to the pervasive character of Hopi ritual art is given by Fred Kabotie, who was born into a conservative Second Mesa family in about 1900. It may be assumed that his early artistic experiences were typical of the traditional Hopi. He writes (1977:8) that before about 1910:

> ...I drew my first kachina figures, scratching them on rocks. And in Shungopavi, other kids and I drew kachina heads with charcoal on walls in abandoned houses. While we were at Oraibi an older boy...and I would go out to find earth colors...and draw with them. That was just play, but I loved to draw.

Kachinas provided the subject matter for young boys whose drawings were "just play," and the iconography as well as the forms of ritual art provided the source material and the behavioral models for secular picture making.

Had Hopi life not changed so radically during this century it is reasonable to speculate that Fred Kabotie's considerable artistic energies would have been channelled into traditionally prescribed modes. In that event his mature paintings would have been done on kiva walls or applied to ritual objects. They would have been made mostly on ritual occasions and would have followed the formal and iconographic rules established by Hopi tra-

Fig. 66. "Home Dance" by Fred Kabotie, Second Mesa, Shongopavi, 1946. Watercolor. H: 52.8 cm. L: 72.5 cm. Fred Kabotie Collection.

ditional experiences. Within the existing artistic system there were (and are) ample opportunities for personal invention and development. Since Kabotie is far too creative an artist to blandly follow any set of artistic rules and conventions, he would undoubtedly have altered the traditional Hopi system even as he worked within it. His contributions would have been recognized by other Hopi even if they were invisible to outsiders not thoroughly familiar with the Hopi rules of art. Speculation aside, that is the way every art system works, and clearly, some radical changes had to happen to the entire Hopi way of life for there to be acceptance of a new Hopi artistic tradition.

As though to prove the point, the most significant fact about the first modern Hopi paintings is that they had no effect whatever on the development of modern Hopi art. In about 1900 J. Walter Fewkes of the Smithsonian Institution commissioned four Hopi men to paint pictures of kachinas for him. Fewkes was an anthropologist who excavated at several ancient Hopi towns during the last decade of the nineteenth century. He was a student of Hopi mythology, oral history, ceremonialism and art, and he hoped that the pictures of kachinas would provide him with a "valuable means of studying the symbolism of the tribe" (Fewkes 1903:13). His concern was for authenticity of subject matter and of native expression: he wanted the pictures to be accurate documents done in a purely Hopi manner. He supplied the artists with paper, pencils, brushes and pigments, suggested subjects but left the manner of execution entirely up to them.

The most prolific was also the one that Fewkes considered to be "the ablest." His name was Kutcahonaûû, or White Bear. The stylistic purity of his work was suspect because he had been to grammar school at Keams Canyon and spoke some English. However, his pictures were similar enough to those of his uncle, Homovi, who spoke no English and had never been to school, to allow Fewkes to gratefully conclude that White Bear's work was "authentic." Most of the more than 200 paintings collected by Fewkes in 1900 and published in 1903 were by these two artists. The remainder were by a man called Winuta, who was also considered to be free of white influence, but those made by the fourth (unnamed) artist were all rejected on the grounds that they showed "the influence of (white) instruction" (Fewkes 1903:14).

No effort was made to keep the production of these pictures secret. To the contrary, they were shown to other Hopi men in order to check on their accuracy and to initiate discussions that would help Fewkes to better understand details of Hopi ritual and religious beliefs. The artists and other participants were initially cooperative and enthusiastic, but rumors soon began to circulate that associated the paintings with sorcery and the project came to a sudden end. Similar associations between documentary painting and witchcraft occurred later at other pueblos—at Hopi it inhibited the production of modern paintings for several decades. It seems clear that the function of a painting was more important to the Hopi than either its form or its content, for the published pictures are little different in appearance and subject from traditional Hopi art of the period.

Most are of single masked dancers or of pairs of masked figures shown in frontal poses, static, blocky, freestanding, with disproportionately large heads and no reference made to an environmental space. In several pictures the figures interact, but relationships are always between members of the group and the artifacts that they use, never between the group and its spatial environment (Brody 1971:78). Figures are delineated with a smooth, even line, and color areas are separated from each other by these lines. In visual character and proportion the paintings are reminiscent of ancient kiva murals and, also, are quite similar to the carved kachina dolls (tihus) of the period. These also served educational rather than ritual purposes and could be sold to outsiders, but they were made to be used by the Hopi and had been for many generations. In contrast, the paintings commissioned by Fewkes had no utility to the Hopi. They looked like Hopi art, appeared to be identical in subject matter and in formal quality to ordinary and traditional Hopi art objects, but their function was so radically different that they could not then be accepted by the Hopi as an art form. They were simulacrums of traditional Hopi art.

The subtle differences between these paintings and the real thing were formal as well as functional. Unlike earlier Hopi pictures made on large vertical surfaces and painted with lusterless opaque colors, the Fewkes pictures were on small pieces of paper that could be held vertically or horizontally. Their colors were transparent or translucent and had reflective and textural qualities that were quite novel to Hopi art. In at least some instances novel compositions, including topographic views, seem to have been suggested by size or horizontality of the picture surface. In almost all, color was manipulated to describe body mass, spatial depth or musculature. These illusionistic devices and conventions led Fewkes to question the stylistic purity of the pictures, but he seemed not to realize that the materials he had introduced may have suggested the innovations that he found objectionable.

Except for kachina pictures painted on pottery by some Hopi-Tewa between about 1905 and 1915, no other secular paintings are known to have been made at Hopi for several decades following the Fewkes commission. Hopi children at the Indian Boarding School in Riverside, California, painted some pictures in 1908, and a teacher at the Oraibi Day School encouraged other children to paint in about 1912 (Brody 1971: 80-81). No Hopi adults were involved in these exercises, and it seems that the Hopi then were in rare agreement with official Bureau of Indian Affairs policy that discouraged the teaching of art at Indian Schools.

While neither the 1908 nor the 1912 incident appears to have directly affected the future development of Hopi painting, they provide good evidence that BIA rules proscribing art instruction at the Indian schools were violated by BIA teachers. Similar incidents occurred at other BIA schools, and the future development of Native American art, including Hopi painting, was nurtured

Fig. 67. "Kachina" by Otis Polelonema. Tempera. H: 48.4 cm. L: 30.5 cm. California Academy of Sciences, Elkus Collection 370-1132.

Fig. 68. "Kachina" by Fred Kabotie. Tempera. H: 43.8 cm. L: 33.4 cm. California Academy of Sciences, Elkus Collection 370-1251.

subversively within the Indian School system. Before modern easel painting could be accepted at Hopi, it was necessary for Hopi artists to be isolated and trained outside of their communities and for Hopi attitudes about the functions of art to change so that the trained artists could later return to work at home. In about 1915, these factors began to come together (Kabotie 1977:1).

> Our village of Shungopavi was divided into two factions that called themselves the Friendlies and the Hostiles. The Friendlies wanted to give up the Hopi way of life and cooperate with the government, to become bahanas, white people, and send their children to school. My families were Hostiles.

After considerable friction an accommodation was reached between the factions, and in 1915 sixteen First and Second Mesa youngsters of both factions agreed to attend the Santa Fe Indian School for a three-year period on the assumption that they could then return home (Kabotie 1977:17). Among them, from Second Mesa "Hostile" families were thirteen-year-old Otis Polelonema and fifteen-year-old Fred Kabotie. As things worked out, Polelonema returned to Hopi in 1921 but Kabotie lived away from home until 1937.

During the school year of 1916-17 Elizabeth De Huff, the wife of John De Huff, the new superintendent of the Santa Fe school, asked several students, including Kabotie and Polelonema, to paint pictures at her home as an extracurricular activity (Kabotie 1977:27-28). Although the De Huffs were new to Santa Fe, their interest in fostering the talents of young Indian artists fit in with ongoing activities in the Santa Fe area. A few years earlier, Edgar L. Hewett and Kenneth Chapman of the Museum of New Mexico and the School of American Research, the painter Olive Rush, the poet Alice Corbin Henderson and other prominent members of Santa Fe's intellectual community stimulated some young men of San Ildefonso Pueblo to paint pictures. In many respects these Indian painters became part of a burgeoning art colony that included such internationally known artists as John Sloan, Robert Henri, George Bellows and Stuart Davis.

Shortly afterwards, between about 1917 and 1920, the two Hopi, along with Ma Pe Wi from Zia Pueblo (another of Mrs. De Huff's protégés) and Awa Tsireh of San Ildefonso Pueblo began to work at the Museum of New Mexico and the School of American Research. All four occasionally painted the same subjects in much the same style. Their pictures were usually documentary, recording secular activities such as pottery making and a variety of winter and summer dances, including kachina ceremonials. Since ritual was so much a part of their daily life at home, it is difficult to know now if the artists considered their paintings of rituals as categorically different from those that detailed techniques of pottery making. In any event, the two Hopi, unlike their Rio Grande colleagues, did not go home for several years, and their pictures of this period are sometimes quite nostalgic.

During those early years all artists in the group seemed to have much the same pictorial goals. Their primary concern was to illustrate, as accurately as possible, things that they observed. They

Fig. 69. "Pueblo Woman" by Otis Polelonema.
Watercolor. No. 176.

tried to draw their figures with "correct" proportions and in realistic poses, to use perspective, to model with light and shade and
color, to paint environments, physical mass and atmosphere, and
to use the whole battery of illusionistic devices that had been incorporated into western European painting since the Renaissance.
They were, apparently, untutored and their paintings were naive
in ways not vastly different from those of other untaught artists
whose objectives were similar. Their visual models were probably the pictures they saw on the walls at school, in the homes of
their patrons and in the Santa Fe museums, and the illustrations
in the magazines and books that they were exposed to constantly
(Brody 1971:85-117).

In about 1921 some radical style changes began to appear.
The Rio Grande artists, following the lead of Awa Tsireh, elimi-
nated specific references to backgrounds and environments and
flattened out their figures by using washes of untextured color.
Perspective drawing was the last illusionistic device to go, but
by about 1930 the "flat" style of painting that came to be identified with this first generation of modern Indian painters had
developed.

These style changes had little effect on Polelonema's work,
for he returned to Hopi in about 1921 and hardly painted again
until the next decade, but Kabotie was a prolific artist during this

Fig. 70. "Koshare and Turkey" by Awa Tsireh. Watercolor. H: 38.2 cm. L: 49 cm. California Academy of Sciences. Elkus Collection 370-1028.

time, living in Santa Fe, filling commissions and supporting himself by painting. Even though his social ties with some Rio Grande artists remained strong, he went his own way. He did eliminate background details but developed great skill in modelling lifelike figures with precision. By about 1930 his paintings had achieved a maturity characterized by active and precisely rendered people shown operating within blank environments whose real space was implied by the illusionistic quality of the figures. His subject matter was almost entirely limited to images of Hopi and Rio Grande Pueblo dances. Kabotie's figures occasionally cast shadows that would more precisely define the "real world" within which they lived and breathed, but that kind of verification was not usually needed.

From about 1930 to 1934 Polelonema painted a few pictures of remarkable strength that also depended on ground shadows for verity and are otherwise reminiscent of Kabotie's first mature style. Rather than being influenced by Kabotie it seems more likely that Polelonema reached artistic maturity in isolation and that the stylistic similarities are testimony that their work had always been closely linked. In point of fact a "Hopi" style in modern art can be defined after about 1930. Other Hopi painters worked away from the Mesas by then, and Waldo Mootzka was only one of several whose style was sometimes frankly derived from that made popular by Kabotie. Homer Cooyama became even more illustrative, illusionistic and "non-Indian" in manner, and illustrative realism came to characterize early modern Hopi painting.

During the 1930s painting was added to the curriculum in Indian schools following the model developed by a remarkable teacher, Dorothy Dunn, at the "Studio" of the Santa Fe Indian School (Dunn 1968). But even as a Pan-Indian style of art developed elsewhere, Hopi painters continued to refine the Hopi style. In 1937 Fred Kabotie returned to the Mesas to teach art at the newly established Oraibi High School. It is perhaps ironic that a man who had left home as a "Hostile" dedicated to noncooperation with the white establishment returned as a member of that establishment, but it was largely through Kabotie's efforts that modern painting was institutionalized at Hopi. Acceptance of painting was finally made possible by significant changes in attitude, particularly with regard to formal education. By the 1930s it was obvious that Hopi independence required the Hopi to learn how to cope with white institutions. Modern Hopi art became more easily accepted after 1937 because it was taught in the schools along with English, mathematics and other essential skills. At least as important was the demonstration that modern Hopi art had potential economic value to the Hopi community. Kabotie paintings had largely been marketed away from home and through agencies over which he had little or no control. In the years following his return he devoted a great deal of energy toward developing tribal institutions to market art at Hopi. Some of the vigor of contemporary Hopi painting can be traced to the control now exercised by many Hopi artists over the sale of their own work and the fact that they can now live at home and sell at home.

But modern Hopi painting is more than an economic activity. During the forties and early fifties Hopi art continued to be reportorial and documentary and, still, Kabotie led the way. His work became even more explicit during the 1940s, as he once again painted precise environmental details—landscapes and townscapes—within which his figures acted. By then he was a facile and experienced artist who continued to invent challenges for himself. His paintings of about 1945 are among his most poignant and emotionally powerful. A few years later, influenced in part by the Kiva murals recovered from Awatovi and Kawaika-a—and perhaps also by the innovative paintings done by Joe Herrera of Cochiti Pueblo—Kabotie made some pictures that are far more stylized than anything he had done earlier. In these, the deep, boxlike space of the Renaissance and the specific subject matter of his earlier paintings were abandoned in favor of shallow space derived from both early kiva art and Cubism and subjects that are generic and mystical. Although he has painted very little since, his work of the fifties predicted the pictures made twenty years later by a younger generation of Hopi artists. Kabotie's influence at Hopi was enormous and may be measured by the fact that during the years he taught at Oraibi, a unique painting tradition grew at Hopi, even though pressure within the Indian Schools was toward establishment of Pan-Pueblo and Pan-Indian art styles.

Younger Hopi artists during the 1940s and 1950s adopted illusionistic reportage as a Hopi way of painting pictures. This attitude clearly parallels similar style trends in other Hopi arts, particularly kachina carving, and it may have helped Hopi art avoid the cliché-ridden formalism that stultified painting as it was taught at most Indian Schools during those years (Dockstader 1959). The degeneration of Indian art into cliché was felt at Hopi, but not so strongly as elsewhere. Those artists, such as Raymond Naha, who developed a synthetic style that combined the precision of Hopi reportage with the bland coloration and other conventions taught at the Indian Schools were saved by a commitment to illustrating things that they had observed or experienced. Most stuck stubbornly to the Hopi style as defined by Kabotie during the 1920s.

During the 1960s the teaching of art at Indian Schools was revolutionized by establishment at Santa Fe of the Institute of American Indian Art. The Institute was formed to counteract the conviction that Indian easel painting had become aesthetically, emotionally and financially unsatisfactory (Dockstader 1959; Brody 1971). It differed from earlier art-teaching establishments within the Indian School system by recognizing art as a professional and intellectual activity that required a thorough academic background. One of the goals of the Institute was to act as a preparatory school in which young Indian artists would be trained to compete successfully in professional, nonsegregated

Fig. 71. "Hopi Buffalo Dance" by Waldo Mootzka. Tempera. H: 47.7 cm. L: 37.5 cm. California Academy of Sciences, Elkus Collection 370-1252.

*"These Hopi painters have been influenced by Picasso," visitors tell me. "No, Picasso was influenced by the Hopis," I explain.*

Fred Kabotie
*Fred Kabotie: Hopi Indian Artist*

*"Our objectives are to experiment and test new ideas and techniques in art by using traditional Hopi designs and concepts as well as our own concepts of the inner Hopi," they wrote (reference to Artist Hopid).*

Fred Kabotie
*Fred Kabotie: Hopi Indian Artist*

art schools (New 1968:8). Implicit in all of this was the assumption that the trained Indian artists would be absorbed into the mainstream of contemporary art. Once again, however, Hopi artists acted in a somewhat unexpected manner.

A few Hopi artists studied at the Institute and at professional art schools in the 1960s and 1970s. Some returned to Hopi to live and work, among them a group of about six or seven who call themselves the Artist Hopid. They are committed to produce secular paintings whose forms are based on ancient prototypes modified by contemporary art and whose subject matter is drawn from the mythical and oral historical traditions of the Hopi. Their intent is to interpret these traditions for the benefit of both Hopi and non-Hopi people (Artist Hopid 1974; Broder 1978). Curiously, two founding members of the group, Michael Kabotie and Tyler Polelonema, are sons of the two founders of the modern Hopi painting tradition.

In many respects the Artist Hopid group is reminiscent of European avant-garde movements of the first twenty years of this century. Members of the group publish manifestos and poetry, and, as with some Futurist and Surrealist painters, it is occasionally difficult to take their pictures seriously because they are so verbal about them. After all, if a picture really is worth the proverbial thousand words why write the words? Nonetheless, the parallel holds, for, as in the case of the Futurists and Surrealists, some Artist Hopid paintings, almost in spite of the rhetoric, achieve a balance between appropriate form and content that makes for satisfactory visual art.

They have made some communal public murals but their medium is usually easel painting. There is considerable stylistic variation from artist to artist but all share the same basic visual attitudes. Their forms derive from a synthesis of historic and prehistoric Hopi visual traditions and whatever contemporary western European stylistic modes seem to be appropriate to the imaginative interpretations of their narrative subjects (Broder 1978). In general, their paintings hug the picture plane much as prehistoric kiva murals and Analytical Cubist paintings did. In a curious way, these Hopi artists have reversed one of the more fascinating eclectic trends of twentieth century European art. They call on the exotic art styles of modern Europe when it suits their Hopi pictorial and intellectual purposes much as European painters drew from African and Oceanic sources decades ago. To these Hopi painters art styles are something to be used as aids to the solution of pictorial problems.

Many other Hopi artists continue to work in the representational and descriptive manner of an earlier day. Visual differences between the two groups of painters reflect very basic differences in their pictorial purposes. The illusionistic artists are reporters who describe what they have seen, while the others are interpreters of complex—and poetic—narratives. As always, good painting is a function of the mesh between appropriate subject, style and performance, and the two modern Hopi styles coexist very nicely. And, among both groups, a high proportion of the artists seem to be committed not so much to style as to a basic professional attitude. It is one that can be identified with Fred Kabotie and may be the most important contribution that he made to Hopi art.

Kabotie treated his pictures as problems in need of a solution. He rarely repeated himself or permitted his work to become formularized so that there is a constant sense of growth and intellectual development in his art. It is these attitudes of professional problem solving that were transmitted to so many modern Hopi artists that have brought them into the intellectual mainstream of modern art. Kabotie may not have articulated these attitudes but he lived them and by so doing prepared the younger Hopi artists to become professionals. It may be that because professionalism was learned so early it became possible for the younger Hopi artists to successfully come to grips with acculturation in so Hopi a way. For, somehow, modern Hopi artists have invented not one but two modern communal art traditions.

J. J. Brody
*Director, Maxwell Museum of Anthropology*
*University of New Mexico*

Plate 1
Village Model with the following kachinas
from left to right: Mongwa (Great Horned)
Owl Kachina) No. 145; Hon (Bear Kachina)
No. 150; Situlilü (Zuñi Rattlesnake Kachina)
No. 97; Tocha (Hummingbird Kachina) No.
142; Pachavu Hú (Pachavu Whipper Kachina)
No. 66; Sip-ikne (Zuñi Warrior Kachina)
No. 48; Tsitoto (Flower Kachina) No. 40;
Avachhoya (Spotted Corn Kachina) No. 101;
Hemis (Jemez Kachina) No. 151; three Koy-
emsi (Mudhead Kachinas) No. 135-137.

*Color Plates*

Plate 2
Hemis (Jemez Kachina)
No. 151

Plate 3
Tawa (Sun Kachina)
No. 2

Plate 4
Sip-ikne (Zuñi Warrior Kachina)
No. 48

Plate 5
Malo Kachina
No. 157

Plate 6
Nata-aska (Black Ogre Kachina)
No. 16

Plate 7
Ahöla (The Germ God Kachina)
No. 116

Plate 8
Awatovi Kiva Mural
No. 9

Plate 9
Marao Kachina
No. 147

Plate 10
Paiyakyamu (Hano Clown)
No. 130

Plate 11
Hahai-i Wu-uti (Kachina Mother)
No. 88

Plate 12
Situlilü (Zuñi Rattlesnake Kachina)
No. 100

Plate 13
Aholi and Eototo (Kachina Chief's Lieutenant and Kachina Chief)
No. 29 and No. 28

Plate 14
"Clowns Getting Ready" by Fred Kabotie
No. 129

Plate 15
Koshare (Hano Clown)
No. 128

Plate 16
"Ong Quang E" (Long Haired Kachina) by Dan Namingha
No. 182

3.

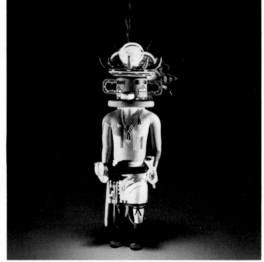

1.

# Catalogue of the Exhibition

The 182 objects are listed below in the order in which they appear as you walk through the exhibit. To facilitate your location of each artifact description in the catalogue, they are numbered consecutively. In addition, we have grouped the artifacts in the major topical areas: introductory statement on kachinas and kivas; the Powamu celebration and its associated functions in agricultural pursuits and raising new generations of Hopi; the spring dances of kachinas and clowns; and the Niman celebration and the associated presence of the new brides.

## KACHINAS

1. EOTOTO (*Ewtoto*) KACHINA CHIEF
   cottonwood root, paint, yarn, feathers, cotton cloth
   H: 29 cm.
   California Academy of Sciences, Owings Collection 520-23

2. TAWA (*Tawaktsina*) SUN KACHINA (Color Plate 3, p. 99)
   cottonwood root, paint, feathers, yarn
   H: 38 cm.
   California Academy of Sciences, Owings Collection 520-81

3. TUMOALA (*Tumo'ala*) DEVILSCLAW KACHINA
   cottonwood, tempera paint, feathers
   H: 45 cm.
   Collected 1962
   Denver Museum of Natural History, Crane Collection 6216

4. TUKWÜNAG (*Tukwunangw katsina*) CUMULUS CLOUD KACHINA
   Third Mesa
   cottonwood root, paint, wool, string
   H: 30 cm.
   Maxwell Museum of Anthropology, University of New Mexico 73.9.5

4.

5.

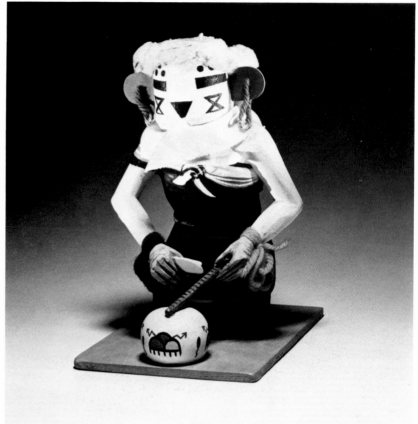

8.

6.

7.

5. UMTOINAQA (*Umtoy*) MAKING THUNDER KACHINA
   cottonwood root, paint, commercial cloth, feathers, leather, yarn
   H: 36.5 cm.
   Maxwell Museum of Anthropology, University of New Mexico 73.9.41

6. WUKOQÖTÖ (*Wukoqötö*) BIG HEAD KACHINA
   Third Mesa, Oraibi
   Jimmie Kewanwytewa, carver, 1940
   cottonwood root, paint, feathers, cotton
   H: 36.5 cm.
   Museum of Northern Arizona 1026/E638

7. NUVAK-CHINA (*Nuvaktsina*) SNOW KACHINA
   Carved 1930s-1940s
   wood, tempera paint, cloth, horsehair, dyed chicken feathers
   H: 29.5 cm.
   Museum of New Mexico Collections, Santa Fe, New Mexico 25592/12

8. NUVAK-CHIN-MANA (*Nuvaktsin mana*) SNOW KACHINA MAIDEN
   Carved 1970
   wood, paint, wool, cotton
   H: 20 cm.
   Arizona State Museum E-8794

10.

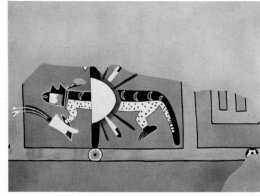

11.

# KIVA MURALS

9. KIVA MURAL (Color Plate 8, p. 104)
   Antelope Mesa, Awatovi, Room 788, Wall E, Design 1, Pueblo, early
      16th century
   H: 124.5 cm.   L: 140 cm.
   Peabody Museum, Harvard University 39-97-10/23099B

10. KIVA MURAL
    Antelope Mesa, Awatovi, Room 529, Wall S, Design 1, Pueblo, early
       15th century
    H: 155 cm.   L: 124.5 cm.
    Peabody Museum, Harvard University 39-97-10/22990B

11. KIVA MURAL (reproduction)
    Antelope Mesa, Awatovi, Room 788, Left Wall, Design 8, early
       16th century
    H: 76.2 cm.   L: 101.6 cm.
    Museum of Northern Arizona NA 820.R.788.12

12.

13.

15.

14.

# SOYOKO

12. HAHAI-I WU-UTI (*Hahay'i wuuti*) KACHINA MOTHER
    Second Mesa, Sichomovi
    wood, paint, cotton cloth, felt, horsehair, paper
    H: 35.6 cm.
    Collected by H. R. Voth, 1898
    Museum of the American Indian, Heye Foundation
    H. R. Voth Collection, John L. Nelson Collection 18/6286

13. TAHAUM SOYOKO (*So'yok taha'am*) BLACK OGRE'S UNCLE
         KACHINA
    cottonwood root, paint, feathers, leather
    H: 30.5 cm.
    Maxwell Museum of Anthropology, University of New Mexico 64.61.140

14. SOYOK MANA (*So'yok Mana*) KACHINA
    cottonwood root, paint, feathers, leather
    H: 22 cm.
    Maxwell Museum of Anthropology, University of New Mexico 73.9.43

15. SOYOK WU-UTI (*So'yoko*) OGRE WOMAN KACHINA
    cottonwood root, paint, feathers, hair, paper, commercial fabric
    H: 30.5 cm.
    California Academy of Sciences, Owings Collection 520-74

17.

19.

18.

16. NATA-ASKA (*Nata'aska*) BLACK OGRE KACHINA
   (Color Plate 6, p. 102)
   Third Mesa, Oraibi
   Jimmie Kewanwytewa, carver
   cottonwood root, paint, metal, feathers, buckskin, yarn
   H: 44.5 cm.
   California Academy of Sciences, Owings Collection 520-84

17. NATA-ASKA (*Nata'aska*) BLACK OGRE KACHINA
   cottonwood root, paint, feathers, buckskin, cotton, horsehair
   H: 40.2 cm.
   Collected by Fred Harvey prior to 1906
   Carnegie Museum of Natural History 3165/320

18. WIHARU (*Wiharu*) WHITE OGRE KACHINA
   cottonwood root, paint, feathers, rabbit fur, buckskin, cotton, wool
   H: 36.83 cm.
   Collected by Fred Harvey prior to 1906
   Carnegie Museum of Natural History 3165/104

19. HEHEYA (*Hehey'a*) KACHINA
   cottonwood root, paint, fur, wool, leather, metal
   H: 26 cm.
   California Academy of Sciences, Owings Collection 520-61

20.

22.

21.

23.

# POWAMU

20. ANGWUSHAHAI-I (*Angwus hahay'i*) CROW BRIDE KACHINA
cottonwood root, paint, yarn, feathers, commerical fur
H: 29.5 cm.
Maxwell Museum of Anthropology, University of New Mexico 64.61.118

21. KIPOK KOYEMSI (*Kipok Koyemsi*) WARRIOR MUDHEAD KACHINA
Calvin Dallas, carver
cottonwood root, paint, deerskin, feathers, yarn, commercial cloth, yucca
H: 41 cm.
California Academy of Sciences, Owings Collection 520-15

22. KOYEMSI (*Kooyemsi*) MUDHEAD CLOWN KACHINA
cottonwood root, tempera paint, yarn, commercial fabric, buckskin,
   hawk breast feathers
H: 35 cm.
Denver Museum of Natural History, Crane Collection 4333

23. KOYEMSI (*Kooyemsi*) MUDHEAD CLOWN KACHINA
cottonwood root, paint, feathers, yarn, glass beads, commercial fabric
H: 38 cm.
California Academy of Sciences, Owings Collection 520-18

25.

24.

26.

24. KOYEMSI (*Kooyemsi*) MUDHEAD CLOWN KACHINA
cottonwood root, tempera paint, string
H: 24.5 cm.
California Academy of Sciences, Owings Collection 520-17

25. TOSON KOYEMSI MANA (*Tusan koyemsi mana*) MUD HEAD OGRE
WOMAN KACHINA
Elmer Lamson, carver
cottonwood root, paint, yarn, feathers
H: 31.5 cm.
California Academy of Sciences, Owings Collection 520-19

26. WUYAK-KU-ITA (*Wuyak Qötö*) BROAD-FACED KACHINA
Harmon Kaye, carver, 1962-1972
cottonwood root, paint, feathers, leather, shells, split yucca
H: 33.7 cm.
Museum of Northern Arizona 3159/E7546

27. SITULILÜ (*Siitulili*) ZUÑI RATTLESNAKE KACHINA
cottonwood, tempera paint, raven and flicker feathers
H: 41 cm.
Collected 1959
Denver Museum of Natural History, Crane Collection 4116

27.

32.

31.

28. EOTOTO (*Ewtoto*) KACHINA CHIEF (Color Plate 13, p. 109)
   Percy Tewawina, carver, 1975
   cottonwood, tempera paint, commercial yarn and cloth, feathers, shells,
      leather, tin, beads
   H: 42.5 cm.
   Denver Museum of Natural History 906/2

29. AHOLI (*Ahooli*) KACHINA CHIEF'S LIEUTENANT (Color Plate 13)
   Percy Tewawina, carver, 1975
   cottonwood, tempera paint, commercial yarn and cloth, jack rabbit fur,
      leather, feathers
   H: 55 cm.
   Denver Museum of Natural History 906/1

30. AHÖLA (*Ahöla*) THE GERM GOD KACHINA (fig. 62, p. 81)
   Third Mesa, Oraibi
   Jimmie Kewanwytewa, carver, 1942
   cottonwood root, paint, feathers, wool
   H: 32.9 cm.
   Museum of Northern Arizona 1106/E690B

31. HILILI (*Hiilili*) WHIPPER KACHINA
   cottonwood, tempera paint, split yucca, commercial string, feathers
   H: 34 cm.
   Denver Museum of Natural History, Crane Collection 422

32. HÓ-E (*Hoo'e*) KACHINA
   cottonwood root, paint, wool, commercial cloth, yarn
   H: 24 cm.
   Maxwell Museum of Anthropology, University of New Mexico 64.61.107

33.

35.

34.

36.

33. CHOSHURHURWA (*Tsorshuhuwa*) BLUEBIRD SNARE KACHINA
First Mesa
cottonwood root, paint, feathers, string
H: 31.8 cm.
Maxwell Museum of Anthropology, University of New Mexico 64.61.146

34. HÓ-TE (*Hoote*) KACHINA
wood, feathers, cloth, string, metal
H: 38 cm.
Denver Museum of Natural History, Crane Collection 4395

35. QÖQLÖ (*Qöqlö*) KACHINA
cottonwood, tempera paint, commercial yarn, deerskin, feathers
H: 27 cm.
Collected 1962
Denver Museum of Natural History, Crane Collection 6219

36. MASTOF (*Mastop*) KACHINA
Carved ca. 1965
cottonwood root, paint, feathers, leather, rabbit fur, grass, cotton, dewclaws
H: 33.6 cm.
Museum of Northern Arizona 3159/E7498

38.

37.

39.

40.

37. HÚ (*Hu' katsina*) TUNGWUP WHIPPER KACHINA
cottonwood, tempera paint, commercial cotton, yarn and string, leather,
   split yucca, chicken feathers
H: 40.5 cm.
Collected 1954
Denver Museum of Natural History, Crane Collection 421

38. TALAVAI (*Talavay*) EARLY MORNING KACHINA
wood, paint, feathers, cordage
H: 36.5 cm.
Museum of the American Indian, Heye Foundation, F. J. Dockstader
   Collection 23/2301

39. SOWI'ING (*Sowi'ingw*) DEER KACHINA
Thomas Takala, carver
cottonwood, tempera paint, leather, commercial yarn and felt, synthetic
   fur, unspun cotton, eagle and hawk breast feathers
H: 50 cm.
Denver Museum of Natural History 963/1

40. TSITOTO (*Tsiitoto*) FLOWER KACHINA
cottonwood, tempera paint, turkey and chicken feathers, commercial
   yarn
H: 27 cm.
Collected 1959
Denver Museum of Natural History, Crane Collection 4829

41.

42.

43.

41. HANIA (*Hon katsina*) BEAR KACHINA
    cottonwood root, paint, leather, flicker, turkey, Stellar's jay and
        Swainson's hawk feathers
    H: 33 cm.
    California Academy of Sciences, Owings Collection 520-65

42. NUVAK-CHINA (*Nuvaktsina*) SNOW KACHINA
    cottonwood root, paint, feathers, felt, beads, yarn, metal
    H: 40 cm.
    Museum of Northern Arizona 3159/E7521

43. LENANG (*Lenkatsina*) FLUTE KACHINA
    Second Mesa, Shongopavi
    wood, paint, feathers, cotton string, wool
    H: 29 cm.
    Collected by Tom Bahti, 1950s
    Arizona State Museum E-10,030

44. KWIKWILYAQA (*Yaapa katsina*) MOCKING KACHINA
    Raleigh Puhuyaoma, carver, 1962-1972
    cottonwood root, paint, felt, yarn, juniper bark
    H: 25.6 cm.
    Museum of Northern Arizona 3159/E7518

44.

46.

45.

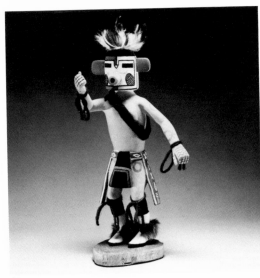

47.

45. KOKOPÖLÖ (*Kookopölö*) ASSASSIN OR ROBBER FLY KACHINA
    OR HUMP-BACKED FLUTE PLAYER KACHINA
wood, paint, barn owl and golden eagle feathers
H: 32.5 cm.
Collected by Henry R. Voth, 1890
School of American Research Collections in the Museum of New
    Mexico, Santa Fe, New Mexico 1350/12

46. CHAKWAINA'S UNCLE (*Tsa'kwayna Taha'am*) KACHINA
Moenkopi
Cecil Calnimptewa, carver, prior to 1976
cottonwood root, paint, feathers, leather, wool
H: 31.3 cm.
Museum of Northern Arizona 3159/E7509

47. QÁ'Ö (*Qa'öktsina*) SPOTTED CORN KACHINA
Moenkopi
Cecil Calnimptewa, carver
cottonwood, paint, feathers, yarn, fur
H: 32.5 cm.
Museum of Northern Arizona 3159/E7511

48. SIP-IKNE (*Siphikni'taqa*) ZUÑI WARRIOR KACHINA
(Color Plate 4, p. 100)
First Mesa
cottonwood root, paint, leather, feathers, wool
H: 25 cm.
Maxwell Museum of Anthropology, University of New Mexico 64.61.135

49.

52.

50.

49. HONAN (*Honan katsina*) BADGER KACHINA
cottonwood root, paint, wool, feathers
H: 36 cm.
Maxwell Museum of Anthropology, University of New Mexico 64.61.48

50. TALAVAI (*Talavay*) EARLY MORNING KACHINA
Second Mesa, Mishongnovi
cottonwood root, tempera paint, flicker and canary feathers
H: 34 cm.
California Academy of Sciences, Owings Collection 520-46

51. WUPOMO (*Wupamo' katsina*) LONG-BILLED KACHINA
Moenkopi
Cecil Calnimptewa, carver
cottonwood root, paint, feathers, fur, split yucca, yarn
H: 43.1 cm.
Museum of Northern Arizona 3159/E7541

52. SIP-IKNE (*Siphikni'taqa*) ZUÑI WARRIOR KACHINA
cottonwood root, paint, yarn, feathers, yucca
H: 34.5 cm.
California Academy of Sciences, Owings Collection 520-9

51.

53.

54.

55.

56.

53. NATA-ASKA (*Nata-aska*) KACHINA
   wood, paint, buckskin, feathers
   H: 45 cm.
   Collected by Mrs. Gladys Jensen, 1960
   Field Museum of Natural History 47954

54. SAKWA HÚ (*Sakwa Hú*) BLUE WHIPPER KACHINA
   cottonwood root, paint, feathers
   H: 26 cm.
   California Academy of Sciences, Owings Collection 520-3

55. CHAKWAINA (*Tsa'kwayna*) KACHINA
   cottonwood root, paint, feathers, string
   H: 26 cm.
   Maxwell Museum of Anthropology, University of New Mexico 64.61.178

56. TOHO (*Tohoo katsina*) MOUNTAIN LION KACHINA
   cottonwood root, paint, rawhide, shell, feathers, wool
   H: 30.2 cm.
   Arizona State Museum E-8212

58.

59.

57.

57. KIPOK (*Kipok katsina*) WAR KACHINA LEADER
   cottonwood root, paint, feathers, cotton, wool, beads, wood shavings
   H: 28 cm.
   Collected by Fred Harvey prior to 1906
   Carnegie Museum of Natural History 3165/191

58. HÓ-TE (*Hoote*) KACHINA
   cottonwood root, paint, cardboard, string
   H: 30 cm.
   Maxwell Museum of Anthropology, University of New Mexico 64.61.189

59. NATA-ASKA (*Nata'aska*) BLACK OGRE KACHINA
   cottonwood root, paint, commercial cloth, leather, sheep's wool, fur
   H: 41 cm.
   Maxwell Museum of Anthropology, University of New Mexico 63.34.61

60. SILAKAFNGOINGTAKA (*Silakap Ngöntaqa*) CORN RUFF HU
      KACHINA
   Warren Kewanwytewa, carver, 1969
   cottonwood root, paint, feathers, fur, hair, split yucca, yarn, ribbon, cotton
   H: 38.2 cm.
   Museum of Northern Arizona 2637/E5057

60.

62.

63.

61.

64.

61. EWIRO (*Eewiro*) WARRIOR KACHINA
cottonwood root, paint, feathers, yarn, leather
H: 32.1 cm.
Maxwell Museum of Anthropology, University of New Mexico 64.61.60

62. SUY-ANG-E-VIF (*Suyangep katsina*) LEFT-HANDED KACHINA
wood, paint, horsehair (?), sheepskin (?), feathers
H: 34 cm.
Arizona State Museum E-4111

63. PALAKWAI (*Palakway katsina*) RED-TAILED HAWK KACHINA
cottonwood root, paint, feathers
H: 29.6 cm.
Maxwell Museum of Anthropology, University of New Mexico 64.61.61

64. TUNGWUP TA-AMU (*Tungwup taha'm*) GREEN-FACED HÚ
    WHIPPER KACHINA
cottonwood root, paint, feathers, yarn
H: 28 cm.
Maxwell Museum of Anthropology, University of New Mexico 73.9.22

67.

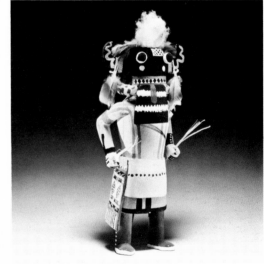

65.

66.

65. TUNGWUP (*Tunguup*) WHIPPER KACHINA
cottonwood root, paint, feathers, wool, rabbit fur
H: 27 cm.
Maxwell Museum of Anthropology, University of New Mexico 73.9.10

66. PACHAVU HÚ (*Patsavu Hu' katsina*) PACHAVU WHIPPER KACHINA
cottonwood root, paint, feathers
H: 29 cm.
Maxwell Museum of Anthropology, University of New Mexico 64.61.200

67. TUKWÜNAG (*Tukwunangw*) CUMULUS CLOUD KACHINA
Third Mesa, Hotevilla
Richard Kayquoptewa, carver 1970
wood, paint, feathers, beads, wool
H: 33 cm.
Arizona State Museum E-8771

68. NAKIACHOP (*Nakyatsop*) SILENT KACHINA
Third Mesa
cottonwood root, paint, feathers
H: 33 cm.
Maxwell Museum of Anthropology, University of New Mexico 73.9.12

68.

69.

70.

71.

72.

69. QÖQLÖ (Qöqlö) KACHINA
   Second Mesa, Shongopavi
   Peter Nuvamsa, Sr., carver, ca. 1952
   cottonwood root, tempera paint, feathers
   H: 28 cm.
   Collected by John and Carlotta Connelly, 1952
   John and Carlotta Connelly Collection

70. OWA-NGARORO (Owa ngaroro) MAD OR STONE EATER
      KACHINA
   Third Mesa
   cottonwood root, paint, feathers
   H: 31 cm.
   Maxwell Museum of Anthropology, University of New Mexico 64.61.132

71. SÖHÖNASOMTAQA (Sohónasomtaqa) MAN WITH REEDS TIED
      TO KACHINA
   Third Mesa
   cottonwood root, paint, straw, string
   H: 36 cm.
   Maxwell Museum of Anthropology, University of New Mexico 64.61.108

72. SOYOK MANA (So'yok mana) KACHINA
   cottonwood root, paint, hair
   H: 21 cm.
   Maxwell Museum of Anthropology, University of New Mexico 66.60.15

75.

73.

74.

73. OWA-NGARORO (*Owa ngaroro*) MAD OR STONE EATER
    KACHINA
Second Mesa
cottonwood root, feathers, paint
H: 27 cm.
Maxwell Museum of Anthropology, University of New Mexico 64.61.194

74. QÖCHAF (*Qötsaktsina*) ASHES KACHINA
cottonwood root, paint, feathers
H: 28 cm.
Maxwell Museum of Anthropology, University of New Mexico 73.9.8

75. HEHEYA-AUMUTAQA (*Hehey'a*) HEHEYA'S UNCLE KACHINA
cottonwood, tempera paint, dyed muskrat fur, waterbirch pine cones,
    abalone, deerskin
H: 26.5 cm.
Collected 1962
Denver Museum of Natural History, Crane Collection 6220

76. HILILI (*Hiilili*) KACHINA
First Mesa
cottonwood root, paint, yucca, feathers
H: 30 cm.
Maxwell Museum of Anthropology, University of New Mexico 64.61.191

76.

77.

78.

79.

80.

77. SUY-ANG-E-VIF (*Suyangep katsina*) LEFT-HANDED KACHINA
Third Mesa, Oraibi
Jimmie Kewanwytewa, carver
cottonwood root, paint, wool, feathers, fur
H: 35 cm.
California Academy of Sciences, Owings Collection 520-26

78. CHAKWAINA (*Tsa'kwayna*) KACHINA
cottonwood root, paint, yarn, feathers, leather, shell, felt
H: 34 cm.
California Academy of Sciences, Owings Collection 520-28

79. ÖSÖKCHINA (*Öskatsina*) CHOLLA CACTUS KACHINA
cottonwood root, paint, feathers
H: 31 cm.
Maxwell Museum of Anthropology, University of New Mexico 64.61.93

80. A-HA (*Aha*) KACHINA
Second Mesa
cottonwood root, paint, feathers, yarn, leather
H: 31.5 cm.
Maxwell Museum of Anthropology, University of New Mexico 64.61.127

81.

82.

84.

81. GAMBLING KACHINA
Second Mesa
cottonwood root, paint, feathers, fur
H: 33.8 cm.
Maxwell Museum of Anthropology, University of New Mexico 64.61.99

82. HOTOTO (*Hoototo*) KACHINA
Second Mesa
cottonwood root, acrylic paint, feathers, commercial cloth
H: 39.6
California Academy of Sciences, Owings Collection 520-51

83. AVACHHOYA (*Avatshoya*) SPOTTED CORN KACHINA
cottonwood root, paint, feathers, cotton
H: 20 cm.
California Academy of Sciences, Owings Collection 520-14

84. MONGWA (*Mongwu katsina*) GREAT HORNED OWL KACHINA
cottonwood root, paint, feathers, plastic, yarn, leather, shell, felt
H: 32 cm.
California Academy of Sciences, Owings Collection 520-38

83.

86.

85.

87.

85. HOLOLO (*Hoololo*) KACHINA
    cottonwood root, paint, feathers, cotton, horsehair
    H: 30.48 cm.
    Collected by Fred Harvey prior to 1906
    Carnegie Museum of Natural History 3165/192

86. HÉ-É-E (*Hee'e'e*) KACHINA
    Second Mesa, Shongopavi
    Edmund Nequatewa, carver
    cottonwood root, poster paint, leather, cotton, string
    H: 24.5 cm.
    Arizona State Museum 74-69-1

87. ONGCHOMA, COMPASSIONATE KACHINA
    cottonwood root, paint, feathers
    H: 30.6 cm.
    Maxwell Museum of Anthropology, University of New Mexico 64.61.116

88. HAHAI-I WU-UTI (*Hahay'i Wuuti*) KACHINA MOTHER
    (Color Plate 11, p. 107)
    wood, paint, feathers
    H: 20.3 cm.
    Collected by Henry R. Voth, 1890
    School of American Research Collections in the Museum of New
        Mexico, Santa Fe, New Mexico 1259/12

89.

90.

91.

89. HOLI (*Hooli*) KACHINA
   Leroy Kewanyame, carver, 1956
   wood, paint, golden eagle feathers
   H: 23 cm.
   School of American Research Collections in the Museum of
      New Mexico, Santa Fe, New Mexico 31912/12

90. HUHUWA (*Huuhuwa*) CROSS-LEGGED KACHINA
   cottonwood root, paint, hair, feathers, cardboard
   H: 30 cm.
   California Academy of Sciences, Owings Collection 520-50

91. KOKOSORI (*Kokosori*) KACHINA
   cottonwood root, paint, feathers
   H: 30 cm.
   Maxwell Museum of Anthropology, University of New Mexico 64.61.122

92. HÚ (*Hu'katsina*) TUNGWUP WHIPPER KACHINA
   wood, paint, feathers, cordage, cloth, horsehair
   H: 29 cm.
   Museum of the American Indian, Heye Foundation, Keppler
      Collection 9172

92.

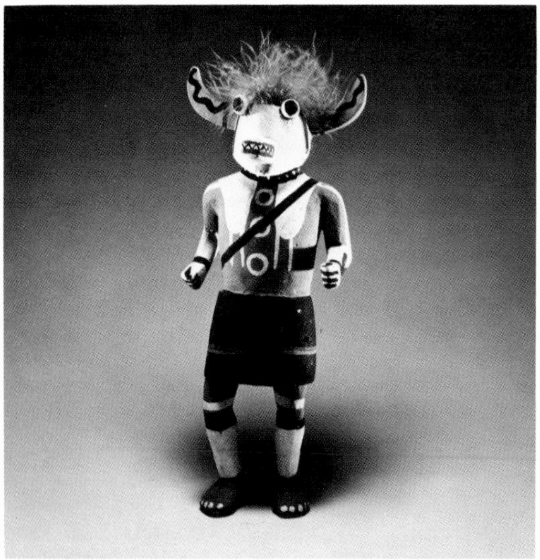

93.

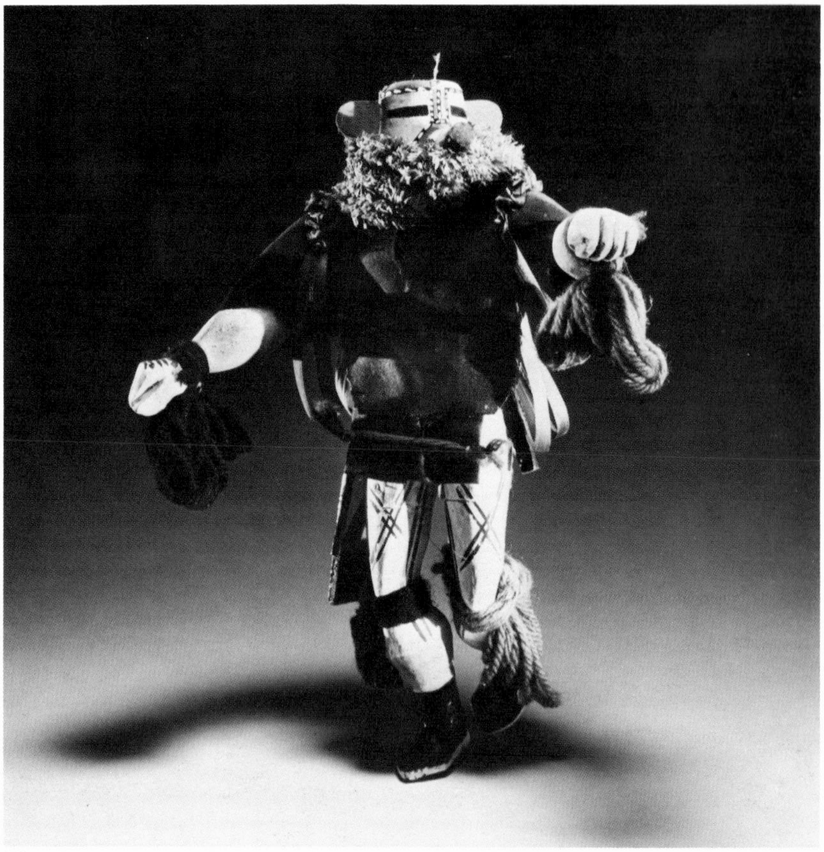

96.

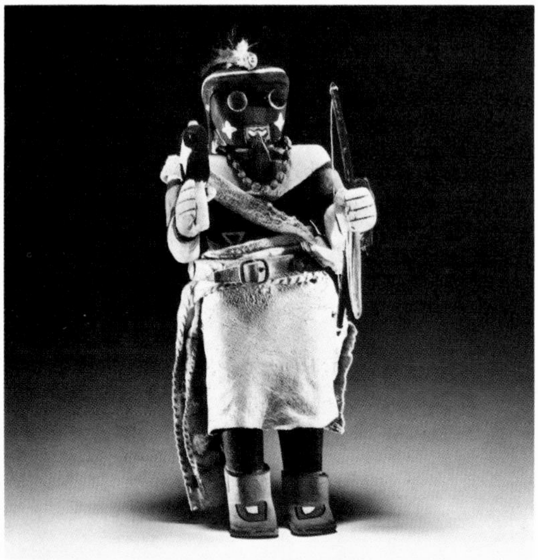

94.

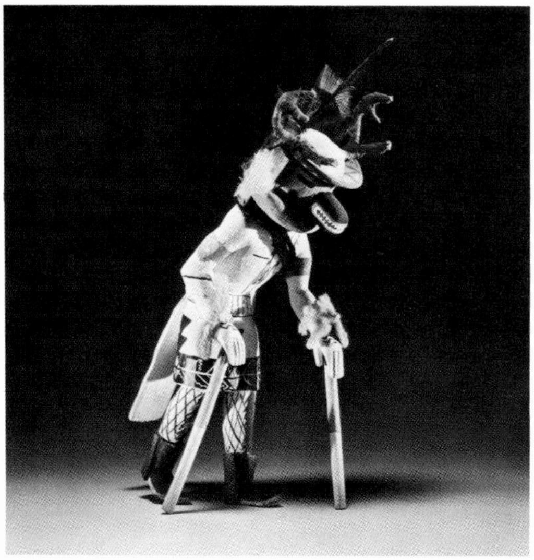

95.

93. OWA-NGARORO (*Owa ngaroro*) MAD OR STONE EATER KACHINA
First Mesa
cottonwood root, paint, feathers
H: 23.4 cm.
Maxwell Museum of Anthropology, University of New Mexico 64.61.67

94. CHAKWAINA (*Tsa'kwayna*) KACHINA
cottonwood, tempera paint, deerskin, leather, tin, commercial cloth, felt, sheep wool, pinyon nuts, feathers
H: 29 cm.
Collected by Fred Harvey, 1951
Denver Museum of Natural History, Crane Collection 553

95. SOWI'ING (*Sowi'ingw*) DEER KACHINA
cottonwood root, paint, yarn, feathers
H: 30 cm.
Maxwell Museum of Anthropology, University of New Mexico 63.34.38

96. NAVAN (*Navan katsina*) VELVET SHIRT KACHINA
cottonwood root, paint, yarn, commercial fabric, vegetable fiber ruff, sequins, beads
H: 27.5 cm.
California Academy of Sciences, Owings Collection 520-59

97.

99.

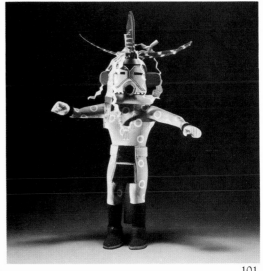

98.

101.

97. SITULILÜ (*Siitulili*) ZUÑI RATTLESNAKE KACHINA
   cottonwood root, paint, feathers, cotton, wool, commercial cloth, yucca
   H: 33.3 cm.
   Museum of Northern Arizona 3159/E7522

98. MASTOF (*Mastop*) KACHINA
   pine, paint, owl feathers
   H: 41 cm.
   California Academy of Sciences, Owings Collection 520-75

99. HUHUWA (*Huuhuwa*) CROSS-LEGGED KACHINA
   cottonwood root, paint, commercial cloth, fur
   H: 25 cm.
   Maxwell Museum of Anthropology, University of New Mexico 63.34.29

100. SITULILÜ (*Siitulili*) ZUÑI RATTLESNAKE KACHINA
   (Color Plate 12, p. 108)
   Second Mesa
   cottonwood root, paint, feathers, leather
   H: 30.6 cm.
   Maxwell Museum of Anthropology, University of New Mexico 64.61.114

101. AVACHHOYA (*Avatshoya*) SPOTTED CORN KACHINA
   cottonwood root, paint, feathers, wood shavings
   H: 30 cm.
   Maxwell Museum of Anthropology, University of New Mexico 63.34.19

102.

103.

105.

104.

102. HILILI (*Hiilili*) KACHINA
cottonwood root, paint, flicker and chicken feathers
H: 32 cm.
California Academy of Sciences, Owings Collection 520-80

103. SIP-IKNE (*Siphikni'taqa*) ZUÑI WARRIOR KACHINA
wood, paint, wild turkey and barn owl feathers
H: 26 cm.
Collected by Mr. Gus Baumann, 1920s-1930s
Museum of New Mexico Collections, Santa Fe, New Mexico 47918/12

104. SILAKAFNGOINGTAKA (*Silakap Ngöntaqa*) CORN RUFF HU
KACHINA
Second Mesa, Shongopavi
Eldon Kewanyama, carver, 1973
cottonwood root, paint, feathers, split yucca, yarn, leather
H: 30.6 cm.
Museum of Northern Arizona 2794/E6379

105. PACHAVU HÚ (*Patsavu Hu'*) PACHAVU WHIPPER KACHINA
cottonwood root, tempera paint, horsehair, feathers, cotton, deerskin
H: 24.9 cm.
California Academy of Sciences, Owings Collection 520-62

109.

107.

108.

# GIFTS

106. HAHAI-I WU-UTI (*Hahay'i wuuti putstihu*) KACHINA MOTHER
    PUCHTIHU (fig. 61, p. 80)
    Third Mesa, Hotevilla
    Ramon Albert, Sr., carver, 1975
    cottonwood root, acrylic paint, feathers
    H: 20.3 cm.
    Grant and Barbara Winther Collection

107. POLIK MANA (*Palhikw mana putstihu*) BUTTERFLY
    KACHINA MAIDEN PUCHTIHU
    Third Mesa, Hotevilla
    Ramon Albert, Sr., carver, 1975
    cottonwood root, acrylic paint, feathers
    H: 23.5 cm.
    Grant and Barbara Winther Collection

108. HANO MANA (*Haano mana putstihu*) HANO MAIDEN PUCHTIHU
    Third Mesa, Hotevilla
    Ramon Albert, Sr., carver, 1975
    cottonwood root, acrylic paint, feathers, yarn
    H: 20 cm.
    Grant and Barbara Winther Collection

109. CHILD'S MOCCASINS (*sawko totsi*)
    Second Mesa, Mishongnovi
    leather, stuffed with goat hair
    H: 12 cm.   L: 15 cm.   W: 6 cm.
    Collected by Charles L. Owens
    The Heard Museum, Owens Collection 630CI

110.

114.

111.

110. RATTLE (*aaya*)
     cottonwood, kaolin, tempera paint, feathers (some pheasant)
     H: 18.5 cm.   W: 12 cm.   Th: 6 cm.
     Collected by Byron Harvey III, 1966
     Denver Museum of Natural History, Crane Collection 8936

111. RATTLE (*aaya*)
     gourd, cottonwood, tempera paint, feather
     H: 21.5 cm.   W: 10 cm.   Th: 6 cm.
     Collected 1954
     Denver Museum of Natural History, Crane Collection 2686

112. COILED PLAQUE (*poota*) (fig. 50, p. 68)
     Second Mesa
     split yucca, galleta grass bundle foundation
     Dia: 15.3 cm.
     The Heard Museum, Collection of Byron Harvey III NA-SW-HO-B-185

113. COILED PLAQUE (*poota*) (fig. 49, p. 68)
     Second Mesa
     split yucca, galleta grass bundle foundation
     Dia: 17.2 cm.
     The Heard Museum, Collection of Byron Harvey III NA-SW-HO-B-173

114. CORN-STYLE KACHINA
     cottonwood root, acrylic paint, yarn, fur, leather, sparrow hawk and
        parrot feathers
     H: 33 cm.
     California Academy of Sciences, Owings Collection 520-37

115.

117.
118.

# FARMING

115. COILED PLAQUE (*poota*)
Second Mesa
Lucinda Palevoyonma, maker
split yucca, galleta grass bundle foundation
Dia: 35.5 cm.
Collected by Byron Harvey III, 1971
The Heard Museum, Collection of Byron Harvey III NA-SW-HO-B-81

116. AHÖLA (*Ahöla*) THE GERM GOD KACHINA (Color Plate 7, p. 103)
cottonwood root, paint, golden eagle feathers, cotton, wool, horsehair
H: 59.69 cm.
Collected by Fred Harvey prior to 1906
Carnegie Museum of Natural History 3165/109

117. HOE (*yoktaqa*)
wood
L: 69.2 cm. (handle)   17.2 cm. (blade)   W: 11.5 cm. (blade)
Collected ca. 1876
National Museum of Natural History, Smithsonian Institution 22983

118. DIGGING STICK (*sooya*)
wood
L: 82.6 cm.   Dia: 1.9 cm.
Collected ca. 1880
National Museum of Natural History, Smithsonian Institution 41695

120.

121.

122.

119. CANTEEN (*wikoro*) (fig. 59, p. 77)
pottery, paint, wool cloth
Dia: 19 cm.   H: 12.7 cm.
Museum of the American Indian, Heye Foundation 22/3703

120. EWIRO (*Eewiro katsina*) WARRIOR KACHINA
cottonwood, paint, feathers, wool, leather
H: 32 cm.
California Academy of Sciences, Elkus Collection 370-857

121. SÖHÖNASOMTAQA (*Sohónasomtaqa*) MAN WITH REEDS TIED TO
KACHINA
cottonwood root, paint, cotton, grasses, feathers
H: 39.1 cm.
Collected by Fred Harvey prior to 1906
Carnegie Museum of Natural History 3165/181

122. AYA (*Ay katsina*) A RUNNER KACHINA
cottonwood root, paint, feathers, yarn
H: 40 cm.
California Academy of Sciences, Owings Collection 520-77

123. SHINNY STICK (*tatsimrikwho*) (fig. 32, p. 46)
wood
L: 78 cm. Dia: 2.8 cm.
Collected ca. 1876
National Museum of Natural History, Smithsonian Institution 23219-21

124. BALL (*tatsi*) (fig. 32, p. 46)
Tewa, First Mesa, Hano
hide
Dia: 6 cm.
Collected by Stewart Culin, John Wanamaker Expedition, 1901
The University Museum, University of Pennsylvania 38629

125. BALL (*tatsi*) (fig. 32, p. 46)
Tewa, First Mesa, Hano
hide
L: 7.5 cm.   W: 5 cm.
Collected by Stewart Culin, John Wanamaker Expedition, 1901
The University Museum, University of Pennsylvania 38629

126. TOPS (*riyanpi*) (fig. 33, p. 46)
Third Mesa, Oraibi
painted wood
L: 10.1 cm. and 10.5 cm.   Dia. 5 cm.
Collected by Stewart Culin, John Wanamaker Expedition, 1901
The University Museum, University of Pennsylvania 38624

127. WHIPS (fig. 33, p. 46)
Third Mesa, Oraibi
wood, rawhide
L: 52 cm. and 49.5 cm.
Collected by Steward Culin, John Wanamaker Expedition, 1901
The University Museum, University of Pennsylvania 38624

131.

132.

# Clowns

128. KOSHARE (*Koyaala*) HANO CLOWN (Color Plate 15, p.
    First Mesa
    Neil David, Sr., carver, 1973
    cottonwood root, paint, particle board, leather, sand
    H: 26 cm.
    California Academy of Sciences, Owings Collection 520-92

129. "CLOWNS GETTING READY" (Color Plate 14, p. 110)
    Third Mesa, Oraibi
    Fred Kabotie, artist
    tempera paint
    H: 74.5 cm.   W: 59 cm.
    California Academy of Sciences, Elkus Collection 370-1215

130. PAIYAKYAMU (*Payakyamu*) HANO CLOWN (Color Plate 10, p. 106)
    wood, paint
    H: 22.2 cm.
    Collected 1920s-1930s
    Museum of New Mexico Collections, Santa Fe, New Mexico 47881/12

131. TSUKU (*Tsuku*) RIO GRANDE CLOWN KACHINA
    First Mesa, Sichomovi
    Alfred Fritz, carver, 1973
    cottonwood, paint, fur, felt, cotton, plastic
    H: 27.8 cm.
    Museum of Northern Arizona 2794/E6373

132. PIPTUKA (*Piptuqa*) A CLOWN KACHINA
    cottonwood root, paint, commercial cloth
    H: 32 cm.
    Maxwell Museum of Anthropology, University of New Mexico 64.61.203

133.

135.–137.

134.

133. KWIKWILYAQA (*Yaapa katsina*) MOCKING KACHINA
cottonwood root, paint, feathers, yarn, juniper bark, felt, string, shell
H: 28 cm.
California Academy of Sciences, Owings Collection 520-13

134. TASAVU (*Tasaptsuku*) NAVAJO CLOWN KACHINA
cottonwood root, paint
H: 25.5 cm.
California Academy of Sciences, Owings Collection 520-108

135. KOYEMSI (*Kooyemsi*) MUDHEAD CLOWN KACHINA
Third Mesa, Hotevilla
Carved ca. 1956
wood, paint, golden eagle feathers
H: 15 cm.
School of American Research Collections in the Museum of
    New Mexico, Santa Fe, New Mexico 44816/12

136. KOYEMSI (*Kooyemsi*) MUDHEAD CLOWN KACHINA
Third Mesa, Hotevilla
Carved ca. 1956
wood, paint, golden eagle feathers
H: 20.5 cm.
School of American Research Collections in the Museum of
    New Mexico, Santa Fe, New Mexico 44817/12

137. KOYEMSI (*Kooyemsi*) MUDHEAD CLOWN KACHINA
Third Mesa, Hotevilla
Carved ca. 1956
wood, paint, golden eagle feathers
H: 23 cm.
School of American Research Collections in the Museum of
    New Mexico, Santa Fe, New Mexico 44818/12

139.

141.

142.

# SPRING AND SUMMER KACHINA DANCES

138. KWA (*Kwaakatsina*) EAGLE KACHINA (Cover)
cottonwood root, paint, plastic, cotton, flicker, golden eagle, and
mountain bluebird feathers
H: 32 cm.
California Academy of Sciences, Elkus Collection 370-731

139. QOIA KACHIN-MANA (*Lwiya*) KACHINA
cottonwood root, paint, feathers
H: 26.8 cm.
Maxwell Museum of Anthropology, University of New Mexico 64.61.62

140. MOSAIRU (*Mosayurskatsina*) BUFFALO KACHINA (fig. 65, p. 85)
Second Mesa, Shongopavi
Carved 1963
wood, paint, hide, cordage, yarn
H: 28.5 cm.
Museum of the American Indian, Heye Foundation,
Byron Harvey Collection 24/3579

141. TASAF (*Tasap katsina*) NAVAJO KACHINA
cottonwood root, paint, yarn, string, parrot and quail feathers
H: 26 cm.
California Academy of Sciences, Owings Collection 520-7

142. TOCHA (*Tootsa*) HUMMINGBIRD KACHINA
cottonwood root, paint, parrot and hawk feathers
H: 35.5 cm.
California Academy of Sciences, Owings Collection 520-35

144.

143.

145.

143. TASAF KACHIN-MANA (*Tasap-katsin-mana*) NAVAJO
        KACHINA MAIDEN
    wood, paint, feathers
    H: 32.5 cm.
    California Academy of Sciences, Owings Collection 520-54

144. PANG (*Pangw katsina*) MOUNTAIN SHEEP KACHINA
    cottonwood root, paint, mourning dove feathers, turquoise, silver studs,
        leather
    H: 44.5 cm.
    California Academy of Sciences, Owings Collection 520-45

145. MONGWA (*Mongwu katsina*) GREAT HORNED OWL KACHINA
    cottonwood root, paint, feathers, leather, split yucca
    H: 32.5 cm.
    Museum of Northern Arizona 3159/E7485

146. WAKAS (*Wakas katsina*) COW KACHINA (fig. 64, p. 84)
    Third Mesa, Oraibi
    Jimmie Kewanwytewa, carver
    cottonwood root, paint, fir, feathers, wool
    H: 33 cm.
    Arizona State Museum E9576

148.

149.

150.

147. MARAO (*Maraw katsina*) KACHINA (Color Plate 9, p. 105)
Third Mesa
cottonwood root, paint, feathers, cotton, horsehair
H: 26.5 cm.
California Academy of Sciences, Elkus Collection 370-848

148. KOKOPÖLÖ (*Kookopölö*) ASSASSIN OR ROBBER FLY KACHINA
     OR HUMP-BACKED FLUTE PLAYER KACHINA
First Mesa, Sichomovi
wood, paint, wool, feather, shell, leather
H: 22.5 cm.
Collected by Tom Bahti, 1950s
Arizona State Museum E-10,083

149. HONAN (*Honan katsina*) BADGER KACHINA
cottonwood root, paint, feathers, yarn
H: 30 cm.
California Academy of Sciences, Owings Collection 520-43

150. HON (*Hon katsina*) BEAR KACHINA
Carved 1964
cottonwood, paint, fur, leather, shells
H: 31.8 cm.
Museum of Northern Arizona 3025/E7198

154.

155.

153.

# NIMAN

151. NIMAN DANCE GROUP
    16 HEMIS KACHINAS (*Hemis katsinam*) JEMEZ KACHINA
     4 HEMIS KACHIN-MANA (*Katsin mamant*) KACHINA MAIDEN
     1 KACHINA FATHER (*Katsinmuy na'am*) (Color Plate 2, p. 98)
    Third Mesa, Kyakotsmovi
    William Quotskuyva, carver, 1979-1980
    cottonwood root, acrylic paint, feathers, yarn, buckskin, grass
    California Academy of Sciences 425–310–330

152. SIO HEMIS (*Si'o hemis katsina*) ZUÑI JEMEZ KACHINA (fig. 63, p. 83)
    Carved ca. 1900
    cottonwood root, paint, golden eagle feathers
    H: 35 cm.
    Southwest Museum, Los Angeles 640-G-160

153. KACHIN-MANA (*Katsinmana*) KACHINA MOTHER
    cottonwood root, paint, feathers, horsehair, cotton, wool
    H: 35.56 cm.
    Collected by Fred Harvey prior to 1906
    Carnegie Museum of Natural History 3165/176

154. ANG-AK-CHINA (*Angaktsina*) LONG-HAIRED KACHINA
    cottonwood root, paint, feathers, pipecleaners
    H: 30 cm.
    California Academy of Sciences, Owings Collection 520-87

156.

158.

159.

155. QOCHA (*Qötsa katsina*) KACHINA
wood, paint, yarn, feathers,
H: 23.5 cm.
Museum of the American Indian, Heye Foundation, E. S. Carter
Collection 24/7348

156. SUPAI KONIN (*Kooninkatsina*) KACHINA
Second Mesa
wood, paint, feathers, yarn, string, cloth
H: 26 cm.
Denver Museum of Natural History, Crane Collection 193

157. MALO (*Ma'lo*) KACHINA (Color Plate 5, p. 101)
cottonwood root, paint, feathers, horsehair
H: 35.5 cm
Collected by Fred Harvey prior to 1906
Carnegie Museum of Natural History 3165/138

158. HÓ'TE (*Hoote*) KACHINA
cottonwood root, tempera paint, feathers, yucca, leather, ribbon
H: 31 cm.
California Academy of Sciences, Owings Collection 520-68

159. NECKLACE (*qalahayi*)
First Mesa, Sichomovi
abalone shell, buckskin
L: 10.5 cm.   W: 9.5 cm.
Collected by C. L. Owen, Stanley McCormick Expedition, 1911
Field Museum of Natural History 83493

160.

163.

161.

162.

160. NECKLACE (*qalahayi*)
Rio Grande Pueblo
coral, turquoise, silver
L: 70 cm.
Collected 1930s
California Academy of Sciences, Elkus Collection 370-1804

161. BOW GUARD (*maapona*)
Navajo, late 19th century
silver, turquoise, leather
L: 19.3 cm.   W: 9 cm.
California Academy of Sciences, Elkus Collection 370-1292

162. GOURD RATTLE (*aaya*)
gourd, wood, cotton, feathers, paint
L: 16.5 cm.   Dia: 10.5 cm.
Collected by Dr. Walter Hough, 1901
National Museum of Natural History, Smithsonian Institution 212614

163. KILT (*pitkuna*)
cotton cloth, wool embroidery
L: 100.3 cm.   W: 57.8 cm.
Collected ca. 1930
Museum of the American Indian, Heye Foundation 22/8917

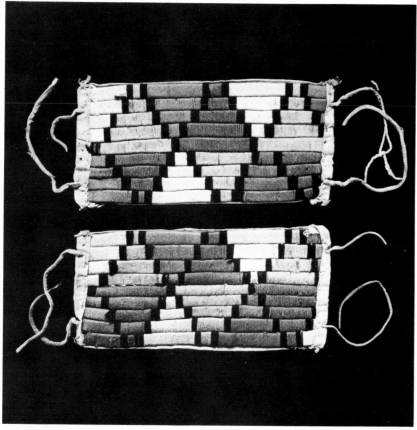

167.

166.

164. DANCE SASH (*mötsapngön kwewa*) (fig. 56, p. 75)
Second Mesa, Shipaulovi
Ned Lomayestewa, weaver, ca. 1948
cotton, wool
L: 127 cm.   W: 27 cm.
Collected by John and Carlotta Connelly
California Academy of Sciences, Connelly Collection 496-9

165. TORTOISE SHELL RATTLE (*yöngösona*) (fig. 27, p. 42)
tortoise shell, skin, dewclaws, tin
L: 14.6 cm.   W: 10.8 cm.
Collected by Thomas Lee, 1897
National Museum of Natural History, Smithsonian Institution 177736

166. ANKLE BANDS (*honhokyasmi*)
canvas, rawhide, thread
L: 27 cm.   W: 12 cm.
Collected 1900
American Museum of Natural History H15186

167. MEN'S MOCCASINS (*Hopi totsi*)
Luthor Honeyestewa, maker
hard leather soles, buckskin uppers, silver buttons and concho
H: 24 cm.   L: 26 cm.   W: 10 cm.
The Heard Museum, Collection of Byron Harvey III NA-SW-HO-C-57

# HOPI BRIDAL COSTUME

168. ROBE (*oova*)
Second Mesa
Woven ca. 1935
cotton, kaolin
L: 193 cm.   W: 154 cm.
Collected by John and Carlotta Connelly, 1945
California Academy of Sciences, Connelly Collection 496–6

169. WOOL DRESS (*kanél-kwasa*) (fig. 57, p. 75)
wool
L: 103 cm.   W: 127 cm.
Collected by Lloyd and Janet Ambrose, 1935
California Academy of Sciences, Elkus Collection 370–658

170. BELT (*Hopi-kwewa*)
Second Mesa
Woven ca. 1935
wool
Collected by John and Carlotta Connelly
California Academy of Sciences, Connelly Collection 496–1

171. ROBE (*wuyaq-ova*)
Second Mesa
Woven ca. 1935
cotton, kaolin
L: 212 cm.   W: 153 cm.
Collected by John and Carlotta Connelly, 1945
California Academy of Sciences, Connelly Collection 496-5

172. SASH (*wuko-kwewa*) (fig. 54, p. 73)
Second Mesa
Woven ca. 1935
cotton, corn husk, eagle feather
L: 272 cm.   W: 19.5 cm.
Collected by John and Carlotta Connelly, 1945
California Academy of Sciences, Connelly Collection 496-7

173. REED MAT (*songoo-sivu*)
Second Mesa
Woven ca. 1935
reed, cotton
L: 185 cm.   W: 69 cm.
Collected by John and Carlotta Connelly, 1945
California Academy of Sciences, Connelly Collection 496-11

174. WRAPAROUND BOOTS (*mö'öng-totsi*)
Second Mesa
buckskin, rawhide
L: 143 cm.   W: 50 cm.
Collected by John and Carlotta Connelly, 1945
California Academy of Sciences, Connelly Collection 496-2

175. TASSELS (*qaa'ö'at*)
Second Mesa
Woven ca, 1935
cotton
L: a: 17 cm. b, c, d: 20 cm.
Collected by John and Carlotta Connelly, 1945
California Academy of Sciences, Connelly Collection 496–8a, b, c, d

168. - 175.

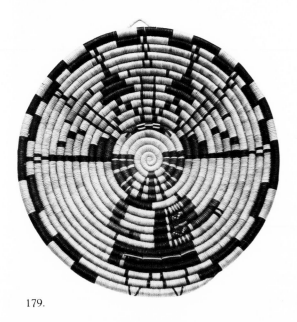

179.

180.

181.

176. "PUEBLO WOMAN" (fig. 69, p. 91)
Otis Polelonema
watercolor
H: 48.5 cm.   W: 30.5 cm.
California Academy of Sciences, Elkus Collection 370-1129

177. GROOM'S COILED PLAQUE (ko-chai-inpi) (fig. 51, p. 69)
Second Mesa, Shipaulovi
Susan Pasivaya, weaver, 1940
split yucca, galleta grass bundle foundation
Dia: 48 cm.   Th: 2 cm.
Collected by John and Carlotta Connelly, 1940
California Academy of Sciences, Connelly Collection 496-10

178. PIKI TRAY (pik'inpi) (fig. 47, p. 66)
Third Mesa, Oraibi
Woven late 1930s
sumac, yucca
L: 53 cm.   W: 42 cm.
Collected by John and Carlotta Connelly, late 1930s
California Academy of Sciences, Connelly Collection 496-13

179. COILED PLAQUE (poota)
Second Mesa
split yucca, galleta grass bundle foundation
Dia: 29.4 cm.
California Academy of Sciences, Elkus Collection 370-825

180. COILED PLAQUE (poota)
Second Mesa
split yucca, galleta grass bundle foundation
Dia: 33 cm.
California Academy of Sciences, Elkus Collection 370-915

181. COILED PLAQUE (poota)
Second Mesa
split yucca, galleta grass bundle foundation
Dia: 31 cm.
California Academy of Sciences, Elkus Collection 370-865

182. "ONG QUANG E" (Long Haired Kachina) (Color Plate 16, p. 112)
Dan Namingha
acrylic on canvas
H: 110 cm.   W: 127 cm.
The Gallery Wall

# THE HOPI ALPHABET

Since there is yet no system of letters (alphabet) which is universally used or accepted for writing by Hopi speaking people, there are any number of systems now being used by those who have occasion to write and read the language. While this work is designed basically to develop the rudiments in Hopi conversation for the non-Hopi speaker, it also offers a system for writing the language that is non-technical and practical. It is a system that is used by most native speakers who write their own language.

The letters used in this work to write the sounds of the Hopi language are set out below in alphabetical order. Along with them are English equivalents or approximations of the Hopi sounds they represent, as well as key words in Hopi to illustrate the sound in a Hopi context.

In this system, the vowels are pronounced as in Spanish, except for *u* (which is like the *u* in English *put*) and the vowel *ö* (which is similar to German *ö*). Most consonants sound similar to the way they do in English. The *q* is a *k* sound made slightly farther back in the throat.

The stress in Hopi usually falls on the first syllable. When the stress falls anywhere else, an acute accent ( ´ ) is used to indicate the stressed syllable. Bear in mind that the best pronunciation is to be learned from a native Hopi speaker whose help may be available through personal acquaintance or through tape recording of spoken Hopi.

Difficult sounds for the English speaker include the following:

| | |
|---|---|
| ö, öö | Make the vowel in the word bet. Then draw it farther in the throat. |
| q | This sound is made at the back of the roof of the mouth (the velum) and the back part of the tongue, and is made the same way as a 'k' (which is made with the middle part of the tongue and the palate). |
| r | Curl the tongue so that the under portion of it is close to the palate. Then, using the tongue as a place to cause friction, expel air through the mouth while vibrating the vocal cords. |
| rs | This is just the same sound as r, except that the vocal cords do not vibrate. |
| v | Vibrate both lips together. Similar to the Spanish b. |
| ' | The glottal stop. Technically, every word beginning with a vowel has a glottal stop in front. This is not written, as it is predictable. When a glottal stop occurs in the middle or as the end of a word, it operates by a mechanism similar to the one produced in the English expression oh-oh. |

It should be noted that *p*, *t*, *k*, and *t*'s are all unaspirated. This means that they do not have a puff of air after them like their English equivalents. In addition, the *t* is made by striking the tip of the tongue against the upper teeth, not the ridge behind them as an English *t*.

| a | a in father | pam (that one) |
|---|---|---|
| aa | a in far | maana (girl) |
| ay | ai in aisle | payni (will go) |
| aw | ow in how | awta (bow) |
| e | e in met | pep (there) |
| ee | e in merry | peep (almost) |
| ew | e in met + w | pew'i (come here) |
| h | as in how | haalayi (happy) |
| i | vowel in beat | itána (our father) |
| ii | i in machine | hiita (something) |
| iw | vowel in pit + w | piw (again) |
| k | as in skate | ki'yta (to inhabit) |
| kw | qu as in question | kwaahu (eagle) |
| ky | cu in cue | kyasen (perhaps) |
| l | as in long | lolma (is good) |
| m | as in may | maatsiwa (is named) |
| n | as in now | noonova (pl. of eat) |
| ng | as in song | ngahu (medicine) |
| ngy | ng in sing + y | Hon-ngyam (Bear Clan) |
| o | o in open | owí (yes) |
| oo | o in wrote | noonova (pl. of eat) |
| oy | in toy | tuumoyta (is eating) |
| ö | u in purple | löqö (pine tree) |
| öö | u in purple, drawn out | lööpwat (two ways) |
| p | p in spot | pep (there) |
| q | a k made in back of throat | quyva (emerge, come up) |
| r | r in measure | kyaaro (parrot) |
| rs | s in measure | kurs (if possible) |
| s | between s in see | suukya (one) |
| t | t in step | tootim (boys) |
| ts | as in cats | tsoongo (pipe) |
| u | u in put | pu' (then) |
| uu | u in put, drawn out | puuhu (is new) |
| uy | u in put + y | huylawu (giving) |
| uw | u in put + w | uwi (burn, burned) |
| v | as in very | iváva (my older brother) |
| w | as in wool | wari (run) |
| y | as in young | yuyku (making) |
| ' | sound in between vowels in oh-oh | pew'i (come here) nu' (I) |

Emory Sekaquaptewa
Department of Anthropology
University of Arizona

# BIBLIOGRAPHY

Adams, E. Charles
1978  "Synthesis of Hopi Prehistory and History." *Final Report for National Park Service, Southwest Region.*
Artist Hopid
1974  *Profile Artist Hopid.* Second Mesa, Arizona: The Hopi Arts and Crafts Guild.
Bahti, Tom
1968  *Southwestern Indian Tribes.* Flagstaff: K. C. Publications.
1970  *Southwestern Indian Ceremonials.* Flagstaff: K. C. Publications.
Bartlett, Katharine
1935  "Prehistoric Mining in the Southwest." *Museum Notes* 7 (10):41-44. Flagstaff: Museum of Northern Arizona.
Beaglehole, Ernest
1937  "Notes on Hopi Economic Life." *Yale University Publications in Anthropology* 15:1-88.
Beaglehole, Ernest and Beaglehole, Pearl
1935  "Hopi of Second Mesa." *American Anthropological Association, Memoirs* no. 44.
Bourke, John G.
1884  *The Snake Dance of the Moquis of Arizona.* London: Sampson Low, Marston, Searle, and Rivington.
Bowman, John H.
1884  "Reports of Agents in New Mexico." *Report of the Commissioner of Indian Affairs.* Washington: Government Printing Office.
Bradfield, Richard Maitland
1971  "The Changing Pattern of Hopi Agriculture." *Royal Anthropological Institute, Occasional Papers* no. 30.
Broder, Patricia Janis
1978  *Hopi Paintings: The World of the Hopis.* New York: Brandywine Press.
Brody, J. J.
1971  *Indian Painters and White Patrons.* Albuquerque: University of New Mexico Press.
Colton, Harold Sellers
1959  *Hopi Kachina Dolls: with a Key to Their Identification.* Albuquerque: University of New Mexico Press.
Colton, Mary-Russell Farrell
1951  "Hopi Indian Arts and Crafts." *Museum of Northern Arizona Reprint Series* no. 3.
Colton, Mary-Russell Farrell and Nequatewa, Edmund
1933  "Hopi Courtship and Marriage: Second Mesa." *Museum Notes* 5(9):41-54. Flagstaff: Museum of Northern Arizona.
Crane, Leo
1913  "Annual Report of the Superintendent of the Moqui Reservation, Keams Canyon, Arizona." *Annual Report of the Commissioner of Indian Affairs.* Washington: Government Printing Office.
Crow-Wing
1925  "A Pueblo Indian Journal, 1920-1921." Introduction and Notes by Elsie Clews Parsons. *American Anthropological Association, Memoirs* no. 32.
Dean, Jeffrey S.
1969  "Chronological Analysis of Tsegi Phase Sites in Northeastern Arizona." *Papers of the Laboratory of Tree-ring Research,* no. 3. Tucson: The University of Arizona Press.

DiPeso, Charles C.
1974  *Casas Grandes: A Fallen Trading Center of the Grand Chichimeca.* Flagstaff: Northland Press.
Dockstader, Frederick J.
1954  "The Kachina and the White Man." *Cranbrook Institute of Science, Bulletin* 35.
1959  *Directions in Indian Art.* The Report of a Conference Held at the University of Arizona on March 20th and 21st, 1959. Tucson: The University of Arizona Press.
Donaldson, Thomas
1893  *Moqui Pueblo Indians of Arizona and Pueblo Indians of New Mexico: Extra Census Bulletin.* Washington: U.S. Census Printing Office.
Dozier, Edward P.
1966  *Hano: A Tewa Indian Community in Arizona.* New York: Holt, Rinehart and Winston.
Dunn, Dorothy
1968  *American Indian Painting of the Southwest and Plains Areas.* Albuquerque: University of New Mexico Press.
Dutton, Bertha P.
1962  *Sun Father's Way: The Kiva Murals of Kuaua.* Albuquerque: University of New Mexico Press.
Earle, Edwin and Kennard, Edward A.
1938  *Hopi Kachinas.* New York: J. J. Augustin.
Eddy, Frank W.
1972  "Culture Ecology and the Prehistory of the Navajo Reservoir District." *Southwestern Lore* 38(1-2).
Eggan, Frederick Russell
1950  *Social Organization of the Western Pueblos.* Chicago: University of Chicago Press.
Fewkes, Jesse Walter
1897  "Tusayan Katcinas." *Annual Report of the Bureau of American Ethnology* 15:251-320.
1900  "Tusayan Migration Traditions." *Annual Report of the Bureau of American Ethnology* 19(2):573-633.
1903  "Hopi Katcinas, Drawn by Native Artists." *Annual Report of the Bureau of American Ethnology* 21:3-126.
1919  "Designs on Prehistoric Hopi Pottery." *Annual Report of the Bureau of American Ethnology* 33:207-284.
Forbes, Jack D.
1960  *Apache, Navajo, and Spaniard.* Norman: University of Oklahoma Press.
Forde, C. Daryll
1931  "Hopi Agriculture and Land Ownership." *Journal of the Royal Anthropological Institute* 61(4):357-405.
Frank, Larry and Harlow, Francis H.
1974  *Historic Pottery of the Pueblo Indians.* Greenwich, Connecticut: New York Graphic Society.
Gumerman, George John, III
1965  "A Folsom Point from the Area of Mishongnovi, Arizona," *Plateau* 38(4):79-80. Flagstaff: Museum of Northern Arizona.
1968  "Black Mesa: Survey and Excavation in Northeastern Arizona." *Prescott College Studies in Anthropology,* no. 2.
1969  "The Archaeology of the Hopi Buttes District, Arizona." *Ph.D. dissertation,* The University of Arizona.

Gumerman, G. J.; Westfall, D.; and Weed, C. S.
1972 "Archaeological Investigation on Black Mesa."
*Prescott College Studies in Anthropology*, no. 4.

Hack, John Tilton
1942 "The Changing Physical Environment of the Hopi
Indians of Arizona." *Peabody Museum of Archaeology and Ethnology, Papers* 35(1).
1942a "Prehistoric Coal Mining in the Jeddito Valley,
Arizona." *Peabody Museum of Archaeology and Ethnology, Papers* 35(2).

Harvey, Byron, III
1970 *Ritual in Pueblo Art: Hopi Life in Hopi Painting*. New
York: Museum of the American Indian, Heye
Foundation.

Hibben, Frank C.
1975 *Kiva Art of the Anasazi at Pottery Mound*. Las Vegas:
K. C. Publications.

James, Harry C.
1974 *Pages from Hopi History*. Tucson: The University of
Arizona Press.

Kabotie, Fred
1977 *Fred Kabotie: Hopi Indian Artist. An Autobiography
Told With Bill Belknap*. Flagstaff: Museum of Northern Arizona and Northland Press.

Kennard, Edward A.
1965 "Post-war Economic Changes Among the Hopi."
In: *Essays in Economics*, Proceedings of the American Ethnological Society, pp. 25-32.

Koenig, Seymour
1976 *Hopi Clay—Hopi Ceremony: An Exhibition of Hopi
Art*. Katonah, New York: The Katonah Gallery.

Laird, W. David
1977 *Hopi Bibliography*. Tucson: The University of Arizona Press.

Lawshe, A. L.
1911 "Annual Report of the Superintendent of the Moqui Indian School, Keams Canyon, Arizona."
*Annual Report to the Commissioner of Indian Affairs*.
Washington: Government Printing Office.

Lowie, Robert H.
1929 "Hopi Kinship." *American Museum of Natural History, Anthropological Papers* 30(7):361-388.
1929 "Notes on Hopi Clans." *American Museum of Natural History, Anthropological Papers* 30(6):303-360.

Malotki, Ekkehart
1978 *Hopitutuwutsi, Hopi Tales: A Bilingual Collection of
Hopi Indian Stories*. Flagstaff: Museum of Northern
Arizona Press.

McIntire, Elliot Gregor
1968 "The Impact of Cultural Change on the Land Use
Patterns of the Hopi Indians." *Ph.D. dissertation*,
University of Oregon.

Means, Florence Crannell
1960 *Sunlight on the Hopi Mesas: The Story of Abigail E.
Johnson*. Philadelphia: Judson Press.

Miller, Horton H.
1910 "Annual Report of the Superintendent of the Moqui Indian School, Keams Canyon, Arizona."
*Annual Report to the Commissioner of Indian Affairs*
Circular no. 433, 32 pp.

Montgomery, Ross; Smith, Watson; and Brew, John Otis
1949 "Franciscan Awatovi: The Excavation and Conjectural Reconstruction of a 17th Century Spanish
Mission Establishment at a Hopi Indian Town in
Northeastern Arizona." *Peabody Museum of Archaeology and Ethnology, Papers* 36.

Nequatewa, Edmund
1936 "Truth of a Hopi: Stories Relating to the Origin,
Myths and Clan Histories of the Hopi." *Museum of
Northern Arizona Bulletin* no. 8.

Neville, Frederica Karber
1952 "Clothing Acculturation Within Three Indian
Tribes." M.Sc. thesis, Louisiana State University.

New, Lloyd Kiva
1972 *Future Directions in Native American Art*. Santa Fe:
Institute of American Indian Art.

O'Kane, Walter Collins
1950 *Sun in the Sky*. Norman: University of Oklahoma
Press.
1953 *The Hopis: Portrait of a Desert People*. Norman: University of Oklahoma Press.

Page, James K.
1975 "A Rare Glimpse into the Evolving Way of the
Hopi." *Smithsonian* 6(8):90-101.

Palmer, A. D.
1870 "Report of the Commissioner of Indian Affairs."
*Report of the Secretary of the Interior Messages and
Documents, 1870-71*, vol. 1. Washington: Government Printing Office.

Parson, Elsie Clews
1933 "Hopi and Zuñi Ceremonialism." *American Anthropological Association, Memoirs* no. 39.
1939 *Pueblo Indian Religion*. Chicago: University of Chicago Press.

Patterson, S. S.
1887 "Report of Agents in New Mexico." *Annual Report
of the Commissioner of Indian Affairs*. Washington:
Government Printing Office.
1888 "Report of the Commissioner of Indian Affairs."
*Report of the Secretary of the Interior*, vol. 2. Washington: Government Printing Office.

Roediger, Virginia More
1941 *Ceremonial Costumes of the Pueblo Indians: Their Evolution, Fabrication, and Significance in the Prayer
Drama*. Berkeley: University of California Press.

Sahlins, E. R.
1962 *Primitive Social Organization and Evolutionary Perspective*. New York: Random House.

Schaafsma, Polly and Schaafsma, Curtis F.
1974 "Evidence for the Origins of the Pueblo Katchina
Cult as Suggested by Southwestern Rock Art."
*American Antiquity* 39(4, pt.1):535-545.

Simpson, Ruth De Ette
1953 *The Hopi Indians*. Los Angeles: Southwest Museum.

(Continued)

Smith, Watson
1952    "Kiva Mural Decorations at Awatovi and Kawai-ka-a, with a Survey of Other Wall Paintings in the Pueblo Southwest." *Peabody Museum of Archaeology and Ethnology, Papers* 37.
1972    "Prehistoric Kivas of Antelope Mesa, Northeastern Arizona." *Peabody Museum of Archaeology and Ethnology, Papers* 39(1).

Spicer, Edward H.
1967    *Cycles of Conquest*. 2nd ed. Tucson: University of Arizona Press.

Stephen, Alexander MacGregor
1929    "Hopi Tales." *Journal of American Folklore* 42 (163): 1-72.
1936    "Hopi Journal." Edited by Elsie Clews Parsons. *Columbia University Contributions to Anthropology* 23(1-2).

Talayesva, Don C.
1942    *Sun Chief: The Autobiography of a Hopi Indian*. Edited by Leo W. Simmons. New Haven: Yale University Press.

Tanner, Clara Lee
1957    *Southwest Indian Painting*. Tucson: University of Arizona Press.
1968    *Southwest Indian Craft Arts*. Tucson: University of Arizona Press.

Thompson, Laura
1950    *Culture in Crisis: A Study of the Hopi Indians*. New York: Harper Bros.

Thompson, Laura and Joseph, Alice
1944    *The Hopi Way*. Lawrence, Kansas: Haskell Institute for the U.S. Indian Service.

Titiev, Mischa
1938    "Hopi Racing Customs at Oraibi, Arizona." *Papers of the Michigan Academy of Science, Arts and Letters* 24(4):33-42.
1944    "Old Oraibi: A Study of the Hopi Indians of Third Mesa." *Peabody Museum of Archaeology and Ethnology, Papers* 22(1).
1972    *The Hopi Indians of Old Oraibi: Changes and Continuity*. Ann Arbor: The University of Michigan Press.

Udall, Louise
1969    *Me and Mine: The Life Story of Helen Sekaquaptewa as Told to Louise Udall*. Tucson: University of Arizona Press.

Voth, Henry R.
1901    "The Oraibi Powamu Ceremony." *Field Columbian Museum, Anthropological Series* 3(2):64-158.
1905    "The Traditions of the Hopi." *Field Columbian Museum, Anthropological Series* 8(96).

Whiting, Alfred F.
1939    "Ethnobotany of the Hopi." *Museum of Northern Arizona Bulletin* no. 15.

Wright, Barton
1973    *Kachinas: A Hopi Artist's Documentary*. Flagstaff: Northland Press.
1977    *Hopi Kachinas: The Complete Guide to Collecting Kachina Dolls*. Flagstaff: Northland Press.

Wright, Margaret
1972    *Hopi Silver*. Flagstaff: Northland Press.